Born In 1975

How Times Have Changed

Elizabeth Absalom, Pauline Watson & Malcolm Watson

D'Azur Publishing

BORN IN 1975
HOW TIMES HAVE CHANGED

Published by D'Azur Publishing 2025
D'Azur Publishing is a Division of D'Azur Limited

Published in Great Britain in 2025 by D'Azur Limited
Contact: info@d-azur.com

ISBN 9798306448541

ACKNOWLEDGEMENTS
The publisher wishes to acknowledge the following people and sources:

Design Amanda Dean

British Newspaper Archive; The Times Archive; Front Cover Malcolm Watson; Additional research Amanda Dean; p12 Apple Computer Binarysequence; p19 (Liberty's Facade) Jon; p19 (Liberty's Sign) James G; p27 (Evacuation) Hubert van Es; p33 Edinburgh Fringe Festival; p50 Vintage Dancer; p56 Science Museum; p56 JodyKingzett; p57 NASA; p57 Salvatore Barbera; p61 Eduard Marmet airliners.net; p63 Wadhurst History Society; p78 Atreyu own work; p78 David Merrett; p79 YouTube; p81 Cédric Janodet; p81 Ken Fielding; p86 Juan Solis; p93 Ethical Trekkin; p93 davidoffnorthide; p97 Corporate Finance Institute; p99 Kingkongphoto; p104 This file is licensed under the Creative Commons Attribution 2.5 Generic license; p107 The Step Blog; p111 Klaviyo; p111 Freshexchange.com; p129 McDonalds; Office for National Statistics; Burger King; p130 Netflix; p131 Alex Needham ; p131 Willie Duggan; p133 Dan Heap ; p133 Sergeant Rupert Frere;

Whilst we have made every effort to contact copyright holders, should we have made any omission, please contact us so that we can make the appropriate acknowledgement.

CONTENTS

1975 HIGHLIGHTS

Monarch: Queen Elizabeth II   Prime Minister: Ted Heath (Conservative) From March 4th Harold Wilson (Labour)

In 1975 the Sex Discrimination and Equal Pay Acts paved the way for a fairer society. Bill Gates founded Microsoft at the age of 19, and Margaret Thatcher became the first woman leader of the Conservative party.

The weather was equally astonishing with snow showers as far south as London in June. The Sex Pistols made their debut in November establishing Punk Rock on the music scene, while on the TV we watched Fawlty Towers.

In September, Dougal Haston and Doug Scott became the first British climbers to reach the summit of Mount Everest .

The Birmingham Six are wrongfully sentenced to life imprisonment and, Lord Lucan is found guilty of wilful murder of the nanny who was found dead at his wife's home.

Mt. Everest

FAMOUS PEOPLE WHO WERE BORN IN 1975

25th Feb: Naga Munchetty, television presenter
2nd May: David Beckham, footballer
27th May: Jamie Oliver, chef and TV personality
29th May: Melanie Brown, singer and Spice Girls member
4th Jun: Alex Wharf, English cricketer
26th Jul: Liz Truss, politician
5th Oct: Kate Winslet, actress
9th Nov: Gareth Malone, choir master
12th Nov: Katherine Grainger, rower

FAMOUS PEOPLE WHO DIED IN 1975

12th Feb: Bernard Knowles, Film director
14th Feb: P. G. Wodehouse, comic writer
3rd Mar: T. H. Parry-Williams, poet
3rd Apr: Mary Ure, actress
14th Apr: Michael Flanders, actor and songwriter
23rd Apr: William Hartnell, actor
20th May: Barbara Hepworth, sculptor
27th Nov: Ross McWhirter, co-founder of the Guinness Book of Records
29th Nov: Graham Hill, racing driver

1975 THE YEAR

Born in 1975, you were one of 56.2 million people living in Britain and your life expectancy then was 72.5 years. There were 12.9 births per 1,000 population and you had a 1.5% chance of dying as an infant, a rapidly reduced chance as this figure in 1950 was almost 3.1%. The 11+ selective exam was almost totally phased out and comprehensive schools were the norm for most pupils from 11 years old.

In 1975, the basic rate of income tax was 35% of earnings. Strikes and industrial action continued to cause headaches for the government, and financial ruin for some companies who had to close.

The IRA continued their campaign of bombing, but the public resolutely went about their daily lives as normal and the government forged ahead with its programme of building new houses to accommodate an ever-increasing population. Councils too, caught up in the fever of new building, sometimes swept away parts of our architectural heritage to replace it with something less pleasing to the eye.

The NHS was starting to creak, though politicians were quick to deny there were any problems, and equally determined to phase out pay beds.

Chopper bikes were a status symbol for children; space hoppers were still 'cool' and there were video games and colour TV featuring Hong Kong Phooey, Fawlty Towers and Dr No was the first Bond film to be shown on British television; Queen releases Bohemian Rhapsody and The Wizard of Oz (1939 film) is shown on British television for the first time.

HOW MUCH DID IT COST?

The Average Pay	£3,380 (£65 pw)
The Average House	£10,000
Loaf of White Bread	15p
Pint of Milk	7p
Pint of Beer	28p
Gallon of Petrol	73p (15p a litre)
Newspapers	5p
To Post a letter in UK	7p
12mnths Road Tax	£40
TV Licence	B/W £8 Colour £18

On 3rd November the Forties Field was inaugurated by Her Majesty Queen Elizabeth at Aberdeen. It is the largest oilfield to be discovered so far in the British sector of the North Sea.

1975 News Extra

January   The Beatles partnership is finally dissolved at a High Court hearing, eight years after they debuted and five years after the group split up.

February   Margaret Hilda Thatcher, a British stateswoman and Conservative politician defeats Edward Heath in the Conservative Party leadership election. She was the party's first female leader, who went on to be the first female and the longest standing Prime Minister of the United Kingdom.

March   Daily Mirror's publication halts after 1,750 warehouse staff are dismissed, after unofficially walking out, causing the loss of half the paper's run of 3,200,000 copies.

April   In the budget, income tax rises for everyone, but a new scheme of family allowances for all children, brings some welcome relief.

May   A coach crashes through Dibble's Bridge in Yorkshire, dropping 25ft into the river, killing 32 people and seriously injuring 14 others

June   Lord Lucan is convicted of wilful murder in the inquest on Sandra Rivett the nanny who was found dead at his wife's London home. Lucan disappeared with a warrant for his arrest and was never found, being declared legally dead in 1999.

July   The completed first phase of the extension of London Underground's Piccadilly line to Heathrow Airport sees the opening of Hatton Cross tube station.

August   The 'Birmingham Six', were each sentenced to life imprisonment. Following their false convictions for the 1974 Birmingham pub bombings they had their convictions declared unsafe and quashed by the Court of Appeal in 1991. The six men were later awarded financial compensation ranging from £840,000 to £1.2 million.

September   The London Hilton hotel was bombed by the IRA, killing two and injuring 63 people. A month later another IRA bomb explosion outside Green Park tube station in London which kills one person and injures twenty others.

October   A murder investigation is launched by West Yorkshire Police after 28-year-old prostitute Wilma McCann is found dead in Leeds. She later becomes known as Peter Sutcliffe's (the Yorkshire Ripper) first murder victim.

November   The Employment Protection Act establishes Acas to arbitrate industrial disputes, extends jurisdiction of employment tribunals, establishes a Maternity Pay Fund to provide for paid maternity leave and legislates against unfair dismissal.

December   The Sex Discrimination Act 1975 and the Equal Pay Act 1970, come into force aiming to end unequal pay of men and women in the workplace.

POPULAR CULTURE

Silent film legend Charlie Chaplin at age 85, becomes Sir Charles, after a ceremony at Buckingham Palace. The film star was knighted in the New Year's Honours List.

Rocky Horror Picture Show

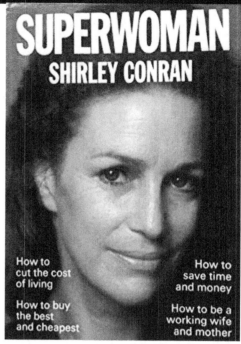

Shirley Conran's guide **Superwoman** a guide to saving stress, time and money is published. The Sunday Express describes it as '*A wise and witty book...Jam-packed with all manner of household hints and endless useful advice...It would make a splendid wedding present.*'

The **Rocky Horror Picture Show** released its musical comedy horror film based on the musical stage production. The story centres on a young couple whose car breaks down near a castle, where they search for help and find strangers in elaborate costumes celebrating. **Led Zeppelin** return to the UK to play five sold-out shows at Earls Court in London.

Gerald Seymour's thriller **Harry's Game** is published and later adapted for television; Agatha Christie's final Hercule Poirot novel **Curtain**, is the last novel published by Christie before her death.

The first episode of the popular sitcom **Fawlty Towers** is broadcast on BBC Two and the musical **Happy as a Sandbag** makes its debut in London.

The National Railway Museum opened in York, with historic and contemporary exhibits, as well as a library and archive of railway related material. There is everything from Stephenson's Rocket to modern high speed trains.

York National Railway Museum

1975

SPORTING HEADLINES

JANUARY Australia's Evonne Goolagong, a native Aborigine from New South Wales beat Czech champion Martina Navratilova to take the Women's Singles title in the **Australian Tennis Open**.

MARCH 'The Yukon Fox' Emmitt Peters won the Rookie of the Year Award in the **Iditarod Dog Sled Race** in the Yukon. A native Alaskan, he won his first ever race with lead dogs Nugget and Digger.

MAY The **FA Cup Final** was a London team derby, between West Ham who beat Fulham 2-0. The match was played to a crowd of 100,00 spectators at Wembley Stadium.

JUNE The first ever **World Cricket Cup** final at Lords Cricket Ground saw the West Indies beat Australia by 17 runs.

JULY Eddie Merckx, the Belgian cyclist in the **Tour de France** was subjected to violence at the hands of the French supporters, angry that a Belgian was in the lead ahead of their native entrant. He was punched in the kidneys by a spectator and fell from his bike. Sustaining a broken cheekbone he had to retire from the race. France's Bernard Thevenet went on to win the yellow jersey.

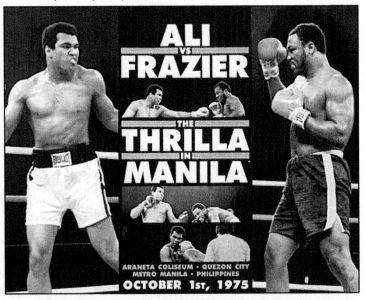

AUGUST In **Athletics**, New Zealander John Walker set a new world record becoming the first man to run a mile in 3mins 49.4secs

OCTOBER Muhammad Ali beat Joe Frazier to retain his **World Heavyweight Boxing** title in Manila, The Philippines. Known as 'The Thrilla in Manila' many regard this as the greatest fight in boxing history.

NOVEMBER Australia beat England 25-0 at Headingley, Leeds in the **Rugby League World Cup.**

SPORTING EVENTS

GRAHAM HILL F1 RACING CHAMPION

In November this year, Graham Hill and five other Embassy Hill executives, were killed when the Piper PA-23 Aztec aircraft he was piloting crashed in low-visibility conditions. Graham Hill was born in 1929 in Hampstead, and on leaving school, worked at Smith's Instruments as an apprentice engineer. He completed his National Service in the Royal Navy, rising to the rank of petty officer and after leaving the navy, he returned to work as a qualified engineer. He was a member of the London Rowing Club in the 50's, contesting twenty finals including the Grand Challenge Cup. Hill did not pass his driving test until he was 24 years old and described his first car as '*A wreck. A budding racing driver should own such a car, as it teaches delicacy, poise and anticipation, mostly the latter I think!*'

He made his racing debut in Formula Three aged 25, then joined Lotus in Formula One as a mechanic, before earning a driving debut with the team at the 1958 Monaco Grand Prix and securing a full-time contract. He was known for his race preparation, keeping records of the settings on his car and working long hours with his mechanics. In 1969 he became a five-time winner of the Monaco Grand Prix a record he held for 24 years. During the US Grand Prix he was seriously injured in a crash, breaking both of his legs. Typically, when asked soon after the crash if he wanted to pass on a message to his wife, Hill replied '*Just tell her that I won't be dancing for two weeks.*' A staunch campaigner for road safety, Hill presented a series for Thames Television entitled *Advanced Driving with Graham Hill* comprising six 30-minute programmes broadcast weekly in June and July 1974.

THE FIRST REFERENDUM

Held on June 5, the first nationwide referendum in British history was held and focused on whether the United Kingdom should remain a member of the European Economic Community (EEC), commonly referred to as the Common Market. Britain had joined the EEC in 1973, but growing domestic scepticism about the economic and political implications of membership led to demands for a public vote.

Prime Minister Harold Wilson's Labour government, elected in 1974, promised to renegotiate the terms of Britain's membership and put it to a referendum. The campaign saw heated debates, with proponents emphasising economic benefits and access to European markets, while opponents highlighted concerns over national sovereignty and loss of control over domestic policies. The result was a decisive 67.2% vote in favour of remaining in the EEC, with a turnout of 64.5%.

FAWLTY TOWERS

This year saw the introduction to our television screens of Basil and Sybil Fawlty. Set in Fawlty Towers, a fictional hotel in Torquay, in Devon, the plot centres on the dysfunctional nature of the owner, Basil, his bossy wife Sybil, a hapless Spanish waiter Manuel who speaks very little English and the long suffering, sensible, chamber maid Polly, doing their best to run the hotel with farcical situations, eccentric guests and very odd tradespeople.

The show was inspired by the Gleneagles Hotel in Torquay, where the Monty Python cast had previously stayed. The owner, Donald Sinclair, on whom John Cleese based his character Basil, was known for his snobbish and eccentric attitude towards guests, treating them as though they were a hindrance to his running of the hotel – he allegedly threw Eric Idle's briefcase out of a window!

CULTURAL EVENTS

BOHEMIAN RHAPSODY

Although reactions were initially mixed, Bohemian Rhapsody has been acclaimed one of the greatest songs of all time, and it is often regarded as Queen's signature song. Released this year, it began life sometime in the late 60s when Freddie Mercury was studying at Ealing Art College and scribbled ideas for songs on scraps of paper.

At one time called 'The Cowboy Song' – maybe because of the line, 'Mama … just killed a man' – he banged it out on the piano, full of gaps where he explained that 'something operatic would happen here'. He later said, *"Bohemian Rhapsody was basically three songs that I wanted to put out, and I just put the three together."* It was recorded between August and September and parodies elements of opera with grandiose choruses, and Italian operatic style phrases.

BARBIE

The 1970's marked a significant shift in the world of Barbie, and it was a time when her fashion and design took a bold turn, mirroring the dynamic changes in women's roles and styles in society. The decade introduced some of the most memorable Barbie dolls, each embodying the spirit of the era, and saw Barbie taking on various careers, from being an athlete to a surgeon.

Barbie broke stereotypes and encouraged young girls to dream big and aspire for new roles in society. This was the seventeenth year of production for Barbie and Mattel decided to capitalise on the upcoming 1976 Winter Olympics in Austria, by releasing their Gold Medal series of four dolls – Gold Medal Barbie and Ken Skiers, Gold Medal Barbie Skater, and Winter Sports.

THE HOMEBREW COMPUTER CLUB

The Homebrew Computer Club was a highly influential gathering of technology enthusiasts, engineers, and hobbyists, and played a pivotal role in fostering the development of the personal computer industry. Its members shared a passion for exploring the potential of microcomputers, which were just beginning to emerge as accessible technologies.

It was started by Gordon French and Fred Moore who met at the Community Computer Center in Menlo Park, a city in Silicon Valley and the club became a vibrant forum for exchanging ideas, sharing technical knowledge, and showcasing innovations. Members would often present their projects and discuss emerging technologies, creating a collaborative atmosphere that spurred innovation.

Among its notable members were Steve Wozniak and Steve Jobs, who developed the Apple I computer, which they debuted at the club. This collaboration eventually led to the founding of Apple Inc., marking a turning point in the personal computing revolution.

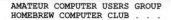

```
            AMATEUR COMPUTER USERS GROUP
            HOMEBREW COMPUTER CLUB . . .   you name it.

Are you building your own computer? Terminal? TV
Typewriter?
I/O device? Or some other digital black-magic box?

Or are you buying time on a time-sharing service?

If so, you might like to come to a gathering of people
with like-minded interests. Exchange information, swap
ideas, talk shop, help work on a project, whatever . .
.

We are getting together Wednesday nite, March 5th, 7 pm
at the home of Gordon French 614 18th Ave;, Menlo Park
(near Marsh Road).

If you can't make it this time, drop us a card for the
next meeting.           Hope you can come.
                    There will be other Altair builders there.
See ya there,
                            Fred Moore
```

The Apple 1 Computer

THE APOLLO-SOYUZ PROJECT

In July, the first crewed international space mission carried out jointly by the United States and the Soviet Union symbolised a historic collaboration between the United States and the Soviet Union, paving the way for future international cooperation in space. Millions of people around the world watched on television as an American Apollo spacecraft, docked with a Soviet Soyuz capsule.

The project, and its handshake in space, was a symbol of détente between the two superpowers amid the Cold War. The American astronauts, Stafford, Brand, and Slayton, and the Soviet cosmonauts, Leonov and Kubasov, performed both joint and separate scientific experiments, including using the Apollo module to block out the sun to allow instruments on the Soyuz to take photographs of the solar corona.

THE CHACOAN PECCARY

By 1930 the Chacoan peccary, also known as the 'skunk pig', was thought to be extinct and the only traces found were fossils. However local sightings four years ago in a remote area of Paraguay, have been confirmed this year by Western scientists.

Small herds are confined to hot, dry areas of the Gran Chaco where only succulents and thorny bushes thrive. The peccary has well developed sinuses to combat dry, dusty conditions and small feet, which allows manoeuvrability among spiny plants.

They are vulnerable to human activity, and herd numbers are already decreasing due to habitat loss where their territory is being quickly transformed into large Texas-style ranches. For this reason, a population is now being established in North American and European zoos.

STANDPIPES IN THE STREETS

The drought of 1975 in Britain was one of the most significant weather events of the decade, marked by an extended period of unusually dry and warm conditions. It followed an already dry 1974, with rainfall in many areas of the UK significantly below average.

The impact of the drought was widespread. Rivers, reservoirs, and groundwater levels fell dramatically, leading to water shortages in many regions and in some areas, restrictions were imposed, including hosepipe bans and water rationing.

The agricultural sector was particularly hard-hit with crops failing and livestock suffering from a lack of pasture and water, which in turn drove up prices in the shops. The government established a drought action committee encouraging water conservation with their slogan "Save It".

INCREASING PROSPERITY

In 1975 unemployment was rising rapidly and job security was no longer guaranteed as businesses suffered under a recession. However apart from the lowest income bracket, an increasing number of the population had credit cards, paying off part of their credit balance each month. This meant that even with uncertainty and static income, people could continue to buy consumables as well as daily necessities on credit. Television was now the major source of entertainment in the home, and advertising exerted increasing pressure on us to have the perfect lifestyle and home, stylish clothes, and better cars.

Women's weekly magazines were sold at every newsagent and filled with recipes, fashion ideas, diet plans, and housekeeping tips they were considered one of a housewife's 'little treats' when she went shopping. Many towns still had a weekly market with a mixture of fresh food stalls, and plants and there were fabric and haberdashery stalls selling everything for home dressmaking, using patterns by Butterick or Simplicity, or with the help of one of the many sewing books by Ann Ladbury.

CHANGING TASTES

Laura Ashley inspired us to embrace Victoriana, with flowery prints and muted colours and Golden Hands magazines and books gave easy instructions on crafts like macrame or crochet to embellish our homes or make our clothes more stylish. Most towns had a department store, and a couple of supermarkets such as Fine Fare, Asda or Sainsbury's whilst in the Midlands and Southern counties you might also have a Bejam store for frozen foods.

EVERYDAY PEOPLE

NEW FOOD IDEAS

By 1975, more people were being exposed to new food ideas, either through travel abroad or through the cookery programmes which were becoming very popular on television. One cooking show that aired in the UK was 'Take Kerr', a daily five-minute series hosted by ' The Galloping Gourmet', Graham Kerr. The show featured a different recipe each day and was characterised by its lighter-calorie recipes and Christian elements. The theme song was the hymn 'This Is the Day the Lord Has Made'. Other cooking programmes featured chef Phillip Harben, or the iconic duo, Fanny and Johnny Craddock. Fanny with her flame red hair and startling make up both encouraged us to try new things and appalled us with some of her strange concoctions, while poor henpecked Johnny just elicited our sympathy.

FAVOURITE FOODS

In the supermarket, Instant noodles and Vesta curries filled the shelves whilst party food included cocktail onions, pineapple pieces and cheese cubes on cocktail sticks, and prawn cocktails with salad cream and tomato ketchup. Black forest gateaux, Arctic Roll, Angel Delight, and sherry trifle were popular desserts. Meanwhile the English Tourist Board was encouraging restaurants to include more British dishes on their menus in the face of our growing love of foreign, spicy, food. One of the final bastions of the English Working Man's menu had to be 'The Greasy Spoon' found at every transport-caff, dockyard, industrial area or area of habitation that was not in the process of being 'refined'. Bangers and fried bread, double egg and chips, doorstep butties and beans were the standard all-day menu, washed down with half a pint of freshly brewed Tetley's Tea.

1970 - 1974

1970:

Jan: The age of majority for most legal purposes was reduced from 21 to 18 under terms of the Family Law Reform Act 1969.

Mar: Ian Smith declares Rhodesia a Republic and the British government refuses to recognise the new state.

1971:

Feb: Decimal Day. The UK and the Republic of Ireland both change to decimal currency.

Mar: The 'Daily Sketch', Britain's oldest tabloid newspaper is absorbed by the 'Daily Mail' after 62 years.

1972:

June: The 'Watergate' scandal begins in Richard Nixon's administration in the US.

Sep: The school leaving age in the UK was raised from 15 to 16 for pupils leaving at the end of the academic year.

1973:

Jan: The United Kingdom joins the European Economic Community, later to become the EU.

Sep: The IRA detonate bombs in Manchester and Victoria Station London and two days later, Oxford St. and Sloane Square.

1974:

Jan: Until March, the 3-day week is introduced by the Conservative Government to conserve electricity during the miners' strike.

Nov: 21 people are killed and 182 injured when the IRA set bombs in two Birmingham pubs.

1974: McDonald's open their first UK restaurant in South London. The traditional café was losing out, slow ordering and service with food served at tables was not as appealing as the clean, fast service and lower prices of this new fast food.

1974: In February, Harold Wilson becomes Prime Minister for the second time (first 1964-70) with a minority Government after Edward Heath resigns having failed to clinch a coalition with the Liberals. In the second general election of the year in October, Labour win with a majority of only 3 seats.

In June and July 1976, the UK experienced a heat wave. Temperatures peak at 35.9° and the whole country suffers a severe drought. Forest fires broke out, crops failed, and reservoirs dried up causing serious water shortages. The heatwave also produced swarms of ladybirds across the south and east.

1975 - 1979

1975:
Feb: Margaret Thatcher defeats Edward Heath to become the first female leader of the Conservative Party.

Apr: The Vietnam War ends with the Fall of Saigon to the Communists. South Vietnam surrenders unconditionally.

1976:
Mar: Harold Wilson announces his resignation as Prime Minister and James Callaghan is elected to the position in April.

Oct: The Intercity 125 high speed passenger train is introduced. Initially Paddington to Bristol and south Wales.

1977:
Jan: Jimmy Carter is sworn in as the 39th President of the United States, succeeding Gerald Ford.

Sep: Freddie Laker launches his 'Skytrain' with a single fare, Gatwick to New York, at £59 compared to £189.

1978:
Aug: Louise Brown becomes the world's first human born 'in vitro fertilisation' – test tube baby.

Nov: An industrial dispute shuts down The Times newspaper – until November 1979.

1979:
Mar: Airey Neave, politician and WW2 veteran, is blown up in the House of Commons car park by the Irish National Liberation Army.

May: Margaret Thatcher becomes the first female Prime Minister of the United Kingdom. The Conservatives win a 43 seat majority.

JANUARY 1975

IN THE NEWS

WEEK 1
"Smaller Bags of Sugar" Pensioners and poorer families may struggle to pay the price rise of 28p for a 2lb bag of sugar. Metrication, will make available smaller half-kilo bags.

"Wasting Energy" Britain wastes more energy at home and in industry than other European countries. Scientists estimate that demand could be cut by a tenth in three years without lowering the standard of living.

WEEK 2
"No Longer Beatles" The Beatles & Co partnership was finally dissolved at a High Court hearing, eight years after it was first formed and five years after the group split up.

"Heating Controls" In a bid to conserve electricity, new Government regulations setting a maximum temperature of 20°C (68°F) in shops and offices and the use of daytime electricity for advertising signs took effect.

WEEK 3
"Ceasefire Ends" English cities are expected to bear the brunt of the Provisional IRA's renewed bombing campaign following the breakdown of the 25-day old ceasefire.

"Dangerous Games" A primary school playing field in Langney near Eastbourne, which was laid out on the site of an old refuse tip, has been closed by the council after toxic waste was discovered in water running through the field.

WEEK 4
"New Archbishop of Canterbury" During his enthronement in Canterbury Cathedral, the new Archbishop, Dr Coggan, took the oath on the priceless illuminated Gospels of St. Augustine which date from the 6th Century.

"Doctors to Strike" The Medical Practitioners' Union, which represents almost 5,000 doctors, has called for a 24-hour stoppage in a bid for improved pay.

HERE IN BRITAIN

"Disappointed Skiers"

Even in Speyside, which is normally bleak, the whole country is basking in the mildest January for fifty years. The slopes of Cairngorm, which by now should be covered in snow and skiers, remain black with earth and rocks.

One ski school has sent its instructors home and told them to return when the snow comes. By mid-January, between four and five thousand skiers would expect to be using the ski lift facilities on Cairngorm, but this year beginners are queuing up for lessons on an artificial slope in the Aviemore centre.

AROUND THE WORLD

"Tasman Bridge Disaster"

A large container ship collided with several pylons of the Tasman Bridge in Hobart, Tasmania, causing a large section of the bridge to collapse onto the ship and into the river below. As the collision occurred on the evening of 5th of January, which was a Sunday evening, there was less traffic on the bridge, but twelve people were killed.
Two drivers managed to stop at the edge, but not before their front wheels had dropped over the broken bridge deck. Fortunately, both drivers managed to ease themselves out of their cars to safety.

LIBERTY'S OF LONDON

Visitors to London are enjoying this year's mild January weather and thousands are visiting the famous Liberty store on Regent Street, both to view the building itself and to shop for the iconic Liberty print goods. The store was founded in 1875 by Arthur Lasenby Liberty, who borrowed £2,000 from his future father-in-law and bought the building. At first an importer of fabrics and objets d'arts, Arthur later collaborated with William Morris and began selling his own distinctive brand of fabrics in 1880.

The shop was completely redesigned in 1924 when a building firm was given a sum of £198,000 to create today's 'Mock Tudor' emporium. It was constructed from the timbers of two ancient ships, HMS Impregnable, built from 3,040 100-year-old oaks from the New Forest, and HMS Hindustan. More than 24,000 cubic feet of ships' timbers were used, including the decks, which became the shop flooring. Designed to feel like a home, each atrium was surrounded by smaller rooms, complete with fireplaces and furnishings made at the Liberty furniture workshops in Archway, London. Outside there is a gilded 4ft high, copper, weathervane of The Mayflower, which took pilgrims to the New World in 1620. The Liberty Clock on Kingly Street depicts St. George & The Dragon and tells us "*No minute gone comes ever back again, take heed and see ye nothing do in vain*" while inside on the old staircase, carved memorials remember the Liberty staff who died in World War II. There are Shields of Shakespeare and portraits of Henry VIII's six wives dotted about and carved wooden animals are hidden throughout the store. Sadly, Arthur Liberty never saw his dream realised, dying seven years before it opened but his statue stands at the Flower Shop entrance.

FEBRUARY 1975

IN THE NEWS

WEEK 1   **"Aid for Historic Churches"** The Government will donate £1m annually for the upkeep of historic churches that are still in use. Cathedrals will not receive the subsidy.

"Levy for Liability" Action on Smoking and Health (ASH) propose cigarette manufacturers should pay compensation for smoking related illnesses, to be funded by a 5p levy on each pack of cigarettes. Ash estimates there are 52,000 cigarette-associated deaths annually.

WEEK 2   **"Indefinite Ceasefire"** The IRA have declared an indefinite ceasefire in the United Kingdom. *"The organisation appears to be working towards a permanent cessation of violence,"* a spokesman said.

"Bumper Mailbag" Margaret Thatcher, the new Tory Leader, received many Valentine cards. One from an astrologer, predicted that she would become PM.

WEEK 3   **"Golden Eagles Back"** Ornithologists are guarding a pair of golden eagles which have returned to an eyrie in the Lake District. They are said to be England's only nesting pair of the birds of prey.

"Ferry Blockade" The Dover car ferry was turned back when 70 fishing vessels blocked Boulogne harbour, as French fisherman staged a 72-hour strike over low fish prices.

WEEK 4   **"Disappearing Gold"** Gold coins worth £150,000 are missing after 10 cartons each containing 500 coins, were loaded on to an aircraft in London, but only six arrived in Toronto. Canadian and British police are investigating.

"Prince on TV" As Patron of the Royal Anthropological Institute, Prince Charles is on location and involved in production of six anthropology programmes for the BBC.

HERE IN BRITAIN

"Pop Exhaustion"

The Edinburgh pop group, the Bay City Rollers, cancelled their European tour next month. Two members collapsed with nervous exhaustion, and the other three are expected to enter a nursing home this week.

One of the biggest selling acts in Britain, with their distinctive calf-length tartan trousers and tartan scarves. 'Rollermania' is on the rise, but fans are having difficulty keeping up with 'all things tartan' due to haberdashery shops all over the country running out of tartan fabric!

AROUND THE WORLD

"Nuclear Hell"

Hidden in Semipalatinsk, NE Kazakhstan, lies a nuclear hell, pockmarked with abandoned bunkers and craters, and an atomic lake known as 'The Polygon'. This was a primary testing site for Russian nuclear weapons, with facilities built using Gulag labour.

Over 400 nuclear bombs were detonated with no regard for the local people or environment. Russia falsely claimed the vast 18,000km² steppe was 'uninhabited', and details of the area were erased from maps for decades.

WOMEN IN WESTMINSTER

Margaret Thatcher (top left), Nancy Astor (top right), Constance Markievicz (bottom right) and Florence Paton (bottom left).

On February 11th, 1975, Margaret Thatcher became the first woman to lead a political party in Britain after defeating both the current leader Edward Heath, and his preferred successor William Whitelaw.

Women have walked the corridors of Westminster in the pursuit of reform and women's' rights for many years. Some are remembered for their daring, others for breaking new ground. Suffragettes were asked to boycott the 1911 census because 'if they didn't count enough to have a vote, then 'neither shall they be counted'. Emily Wilding Davison chose to hide in a Westminster broom cupboard on that night to avoid appearing on any census form and was discovered by cleaners next morning.

Women aged 30 were given the vote in 1918 after World War I, in time for the General Election. The first woman to be elected to the House of Commons was Constance Markievicz, an Irish nationalist and revolutionary. A founding member of the Irish Citizen Army she took part in the Easter Rising of 1916, but as she was in Holloway Prison at the time of her election, she never took her seat. The first woman to actually take her seat in parliament, in 1919, was Nancy, Viscountess Astor, whose 2nd marriage gave her a title and a taste for politics. She represented Plymouth Sutton until 1945. Florence Paton she became the first woman to chair a debate on the Floor of the House of Commons in 1948. Margaret Bondfield was made the first female cabinet minister, and privy counsellor in 1929, and just after WWII became the first woman to preside over the whole House of Commons as Chairman of Committees, although she didn't occupy the Speaker's Chair. This privilege was not given to a woman until 1970 when Margaret Anderson became Deputy Speaker.

MARCH 1975

IN THE NEWS

WEEK 1   **"Refuse Tips Risk"** Uncollected refuse piling up in Glasgow city centre at the rate of a thousand tons a day, has become a serious health hazard as the strike is now 7 weeks old.

"Flood Prevention" Civil engineers can now design flood protection schemes, thanks to research work by a government team set up five years ago, to investigate ways of forecasting sporadic floods.

WEEK 2   **"Strike Costs Jobs"** British Leyland strikers may face redundancy when the strike ends. The company has lost a £2m contract from Korea.

"Airlines Want More Concordes" British and French aircraft industries are pressing for six additional Concorde supersonic airliners to be built.

WEEK 3   **"Rush to Beat the Post"** The Post Office handled piles of extra mail as people rushed to beat the newly introduced 7p first-class letter postage rate.

"Teacher Redundancies" Richmond's Council is to cut £1m from the education budget making 200 teachers redundant, after talks with national teachers unions.

WEEK 4   **"Sell by Dates"** Legislation will require food processors and shopkeepers to show, on packets of pre-packed foods, the dates by which they should be sold. White sugar, fresh, fruit and vegetables, and frozen products are exempt.

"North Wind Doth Blow" An Arctic air stream swept across the country this Easter weekend causing Heathrow airport to close for two hours to clear the snow.

HERE IN BRITAIN

"Trudeau in Town"

Mr Pierre Trudeau, the Canadian Prime Minister, inspected a guard of honour of the Honourable Artillery Company at Guildhall before he received the Freedom of the City of London, one of the oldest surviving traditional ceremonies still in existence, and an honour which is only open to Commonwealth and British citizens.

Traditionally but apocryphally associated with freemen rights, include the right to drive sheep and cattle over London Bridge and carry a naked sword in public.

AROUND THE WORLD

"Doctor Yellow"

'Doctor Yellow' is the nickname for high-speed diagnostic trains that are used on the Bullet train lines in Japan. They have a distinctive yellow livery giving rise to the name and are fitted with electronic equipment to monitor the condition of the track and overhead cables.

Line inspections are carried out regularly at full speed, up to 270 km/h or 168 mph but because the schedule for this train is not publicised, witnessing a Doctor Yellow in operation is by pure chance. As a result, seeing one is believed to bring the viewer good luck.

OUR DEBT TO THE RNLI

Nine Lifeboat Stations mark 150 years' service this year; Appledore, Courtmacsherry, Cromer, Dun Laoghaire, Hartlepool, Howth, Newcastle Co. Down, Padstow and Skegness. And yet perhaps because lifeboatmen are characteristically modest about their work, perhaps because the service they perform makes no financial demands on the ratepayer or taxpayer, many people seem unaware of the hundreds of lives they save each year and the risks they undergo. The lifeboat is expected to be at hand when needed, like the police car, the fire engine or the ambulance. The lifeboat is expected to be on hand when needed, like police cars, fire engines or ambulances. That the Royal National Life-boat Institution is supported entirely by voluntary subscriptions probably only occurs to the average person for a few moments a year when he sees a collection box or a poster appealing for funds.

Yet in coastal towns and villages the threat of disaster at sea is more imminent, the lifeboat service is more familiar and volunteers to man the boats continue to come forward amidst the changing nature of the services they have been called on to perform in recent years. The decline of the fishing industry in many parts of the country has been accompanied by a phenomenal increase in the number of pleasure-boat owners, out in force during the main holiday months of July, August and September.

As an official put it, the institution's charter is to rescue people from the sea without distinction between nationalities or circumstances and this includes *'bloody fools'* as much as those who are victims of an Act of God. A glance at the accounts of rescues in the institution's quarterly journal will convince both the unfortunate and the foolish how great is their debt to those who uncomplainingly risk their lives to save others.

APRIL 1975

IN THE NEWS

WEEK 1 **"Fish Prices Up"** Some retail fish prices have risen by half because of the inshore fishermen's blockade of English and Scottish ports. Varieties such as whiting, herring and mackerel may soon become scarce.

"Resistance to Diets" Scientists have proved that prolonged dieting can lead to a drop in the body's need for food meaning that a standard reducing diet no longer has any effect.

WEEK 2 **"Cairngorms Blizzard"** Severe blizzards swept the Cairngorms and holidaymakers were kept from the ski slopes by high winds and heavy snow.

"Live Exports" The Ministry of Agriculture is to tighten regulations in the live export of animals, due to allegations of cruelty to sheep exported to France.

WEEK 3 **"A New Star"** A new type of star has been discovered by astronomers from universities in London and Birmingham. It was discovered using the British satellite known as 'Ariel-S'.

"Fighting Water Pollution" Awards for Industry have been given to five British and two international companies for schemes to reduce water pollution. The gold medal was won by the Scottish Distillers Company.

WEEK 4 **"Thanksgiving Service"** The Queen attended a service of thanksgiving on St. George's Day with members of the Royal Family, at St George's Chapel, Windsor, to celebrate the 500th Anniversary of its construction.

"High Price to Pay" The annual cost of running the average family car has risen by nearly £240 in the past year, which for many is more than the house mortgage repayments.

HERE IN BRITAIN

"Rough, Tough, Budget"

Denis Healey posed for photographers on the steps of No.11 Downing Street, with the red leather dispatch box. He delivered a "rough, tough" Spring budget, raising taxes, cutting spending, and higher duty on alcohol, cigarettes and bingo.

The leader of the opposition, Margaret Thatcher, called it a genuine socialist budget, 'equal shares of misery for all'. A suspicious object on a Foreign Office windowsill overlooking Downing Street, was found by police to be someone's packed lunch!

AROUND THE WORLD

"Microsoft Born"

'Popular Electronics' ran a feature on the Altair 8800 microcomputer which inspired childhood friends Bill Gates and Paul Allen to set up a business using their skills in computer programming.

They submitted to the computer company MITS, that they could program a BASIC (Beginners' All-purpose Symbolic Instruction Code) interpreter for the Altair 8800 which they successfully demonstrated. Gates and Allen then established their own company, Microsoft.

THE EAGLE

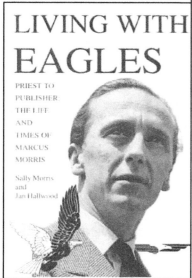

25 years ago this month, the most famous of Marcus Morris's publications, 'The Eagle' comic went on sale. Born in Preston, Lancashire the son of a clergyman, Morris became an Anglican Priest in 1940 and from the beginning, he published Christian magazines for his younger parishioners, illustrated by Frank Hampson. He was part of a group of editors who formed the Society of Christian Publicity, and wrote an article entitled "Comics that bring Horror into the Nursery", decrying the violence of American crime and horror comics. He was impressed by the high standard of artwork but disgusted by their content. Realising a market existed for a children's comic featuring cartoon action stories but conveying Christian standards and morals, he and Hampson produced The Eagle.

The comic was enormously successful, the first issue selling 900,000 copies. The full colour cover featured the iconic *"Dan Dare, Pilot of The Future"*, created by Hampson, which was the UK's first science-fiction comic strip of any significance. Other popular stories included *"Riders of the Range"* and *"PC. 49"*. Eagle also contained news, sport sections, and educational cutaway diagrams of sophisticated machinery, the first of which, detailed the inner workings of the British Rail 18000 locomotive.

A member's club was created, and a range of related merchandise licensed for sale. The comic was heavily publicised before its release; copies were mailed direct to several hundred thousand people who worked with children, and a "Hunt the Eagle" scheme was launched, whereby large papier-mâché golden eagles were set on top of several Humber Hawk cars, and toured across Britain. Those who spotted an eagle were offered tokens worth 3d which could be exchanged for a free copy.

MAY 1975

IN THE NEWS

WEEK 1   **"Wild Birds Protest"** 600,000 wild birds are imported into Britain annually. The RSPB criticises the conditions in which they are trapped and is calling for a Government ban.

"New Paper for Scotland" The first edition of the Scottish Daily News has rolled off the press in Glasgow, watched by the Secretary of State for Industry, and Robert Maxwell.

WEEK 2   **"Channel Island Celebrations"** An exhibition opened at the Imperial War Museum to celebrate the thirtieth anniversary of the Islands' liberation from German occupation.

"Old Attitude" The agriculture minister has criticised those who believe that Britain can find adequate and cheap food supplies outside the EEC. The idea that Commonwealth countries would *'queue up to meet our needs if we left the Community'* revealed *'an outmoded attitude.'*

WEEK 3   **"Blood Trade"** The World Health Organization has expressed concern over the extensive trade in human blood, which is sold by the poor in underdeveloped countries for export.

"Radio 1 "Roadshow Disaster" 39 people received hospital treatment following a crush of fans at the Radio One Road Show. The Bay City Rollers left without performing.

WEEK 4   **"Medical Loss Causing Concern"** In the past year 284 hospital consultants and 40 senior registrars have emigrated. Most leave for Canada, with others going to America, Australia, New Zealand and Saudi Arabia.

"Coach Crash" A coach crashed through the side of Dibble's Bridge in Yorkshire, dropping 25ft to the river below. The accident happened just outside Hebden Bridge, on the Grassington Road. 32 people were killed and 14 seriously injured.

HERE IN BRITAIN

"Whittington Walks"

A group of London mayors, and mayoresses, dressed in traditional ceremonial attire, including fur-trimmed red cloaks, black hats and heavy gold chains, began their annual five-mile charity walk from Highgate Hill at the statue of Dick Whittington and his cat to the Mansion House.

This commemorates the 'turning again' of Dick Whittington before he became Lord Mayor of London. The London Pearly Kings' and Queens' Society, one of London's oldest charities, accompanied the councillors.

AROUND THE WORLD

"Giant Hailstones in Tennessee"

During a recent storm, hail stones as large as tennis balls hit Wernerville, TN. Farmers affected by the hail are now evaluating the extent of damage to their crops and determining if replanting will be necessary. The whole state is prone to thunderstorms, tornadoes, and hurricanes.

When hail reaches 2 inches or larger in diameter, it is classed as 'Significant Severe Hail' which coupled with winds of 75 mph or higher, can cause considerable damage.

THE FALL OF SAIGON

SURRENDER!

Saigon Yields Unconditionally; End Comes Only Hours After Last Americans Fly Out

On the 30th April, South Vietnamese President Duong Van Minh announced an unconditional surrender, asking his forces to lay down their arms. In a radio address to the Vietcong he said, "*We are here to hand over to you the power in order to avoid bloodshed,*" and appealed to them to halt all hostilities, bringing 35 years of fighting in South Vietnam to an end.

Swarms of helicopters lifted thousands of Americans and Vietnamese military and civilian personnel from Saigon in the final withdrawal from Vietnam. Twenty years of United States involvement ended in scenes of chaos as weeping Vietnamese pleaded for places in evacuation convoys and tried to force their way into the American Embassy. American Marine and civilian helicopters, flying in groups of three, plucked evacuees from the top of the embassy building and ledges of blocks of flats. The evacuation began after a Vietcong demand, agreed to by President Duong Van Minh, that all Americans leave the country within 24 hours, the withdrawal of the United States Seventh Fleet from Vietnam waters and the disarming of Saigon's army and police.

Meanwhile in the streets, looting broke out - two policemen were seen putting their weapons into a chest of drawers to be able to cart it away more easily, while small boys struggled to carry away armchairs.Helicopters were ditched wholesale into the sea in the frantic evacuation. In the first 90 minutes of the operation, 14 helicopters carrying among others, Air Vice-Marshal Nguyen Cao Ky, the former vice-president, landed on the small helicopter pad on the back of the command ship Blue Ridge, and were then dumped, after discharging their passengers, into the sea to make room for more, while rescue boats sped around the ship to fish out the helicopter pilots.

JUNE 1975

IN THE NEWS

WEEK 1   **"Aspro Jobs Lost"** 120 members of the staff at Slough's Aspro-Nicholas research plant are being made redundant following the company's decision to relocate to Paris.

"Snowdon Wearing Away" Snowdon is being eroded by the vast number of visitors. It has been recommended that the whole area should be managed by a special committee.

WEEK 2   **"County Closes School"** Durham County Council have challenged the NUT advice to teachers not to teach disruptive pupils, by closing a 1,000-pupil school where staff are following the Union's advice.

"Mine Explosion" The Coal Board closed the faces at Houghton Main colliery in South Yorkshire, where an explosion has killed five men. The Energy Secretary reminded people of the dangerous price of providing coal.

WEEK 3   **"Lord Lucan Accused"** Lady Lucan identified her husband as her assailant who tried to strangle her in their home on the night their children's nursemaid was found dead.

"Beagles Stolen" Two beagles used in experiments with cigarettes, have been stolen by Animal Rights activists, who informed the press *"One of the dogs coughed and wheezed like a human being who has smoked for 30 years"*

WEEK 4   **"Save The Whales"** Delegates of The International Whaling Council met in London to set limits on the hunting of whales. Peter Scott warned whales are on the brink of extinction.

"County Hospital – A Medical Slum" Doctors at the Royal Hampshire County Hospital in Winchester complained in an open letter of *'the medically dangerous conditions of a 19th century Building'* describing it as a medical slum.

HERE IN BRITAIN

"Snow Falls on London"

This week saw the first snow and sleet to fall across all parts of the country in summer since 1888. An inch of snow covered the cricket pitch at Buxton and snowflakes fell briefly on Lord's cricket ground in London.

Arctic winds swept across the UK with 3.3C recorded in Scotland, more like the depths of winter than early summer. Sleet was reported as far south as Portsmouth. It melted quickly across the South but lingered on the ground for days in parts of Scotland.

AROUND THE WORLD

"Open-Rear Buses in Paris"

This summer it will be possible to ride on the open rear platform of a Paris bus again, after the practice was abolished in early 1971. The new, old-style buses are being re-introduced to please both Parisians and tourists.

There will be one difference - the chains which used to let the adventurous leap on and off the rear platform have gone. Access will now be only through the bus, which, considering the speed and volume of Paris traffic, is probably a wise safety precaution.

NATIONAL GARDEN SCHEME

The National Garden Scheme is a charity which raises millions of pounds each year for nursing and health charities, community gardens, and other causes by giving visitors unique access to many exceptional private gardens in the UK. One special garden which opened for just one day in June is Choumert Square. Although it is called 'Square', it is actually a narrow lane-way of 46 tiny cottages and tiny gardens of a secret Southwark street. They have evolved over some 40 years, triggered initially by a few residents' passion for gardening that infused the enthusiasm of others, and they are now a famous London landmark.

The Square was named after the Frenchman, George Choumert who owned the land, and in the 19th Century, had these artisan cottages built. The 1891 Census lists the various occupations of the 106 residents, from bricklayer, dressmaker, and bookbinder, to carpenter, pastry cook and steam engine fitter.

Today the properties are classed as either single occupancy or for a couple, but in the same 1891 census one little house on the North side was home to at least 6 people. Back then, Choumert Square was known to locals as Cut-Throat Lane, so it was obviously far less salubrious than today. Plants seem to thrive in the soil here as it is very rich from past generations when the land was used for market gardening. Today, the Square gardens demonstrate how gardening can unite a community. The street divides into a sunny side and a shady side, which is reflected in the planting. A wide variety of roses provide colour for much of the year against a backdrop of a mixture of trees including birch, willow, and eucalyptus whilst pots are filled with a colourful array of perennial border plants and annuals.

JULY 1975

IN THE NEWS

WEEK 1   **"Below the Mark"** 60% of the doctors from overseas failed the General Medical Council's first compulsory language and medical competence tests.

"Magna Carta on Loan" For the bicentennial celebrations of American independence, this year, the British Library is to lend to the United States Congress, one of its four original copies of the Magna Carta.

WEEK 2   **"Leaving School Early"** Proposals have been made to allow all pupils who are 16 to leave school at the spring Bank holiday instead of waiting until the end of the summer term.

"Roadside Savings" To save up to £1m, the Department of the Environment will stop cutting grass on motorways and trunk roads, except if vegetation impedes visibility.

WEEK 3   **"Court Will Sit Late"** The court at Bow Street, will be kept open until late for the arrival from Australia of the runaway MP John Stonehouse, and secretary, Sheila Buckley, to face charges of fraud, theft and conspiracy.

"Butter Production Stopped" An increasing shortage of milk due to poor grass growth, and increased slaughter of dairy cattle, has led the Milk Marketing Board to call for a halt to production of butter for the foreseeable future.

WEEK 4   **"Road Maintenance Cuts"** Spending on trunk road maintenance will be cut by 20% by surface dressings rather than resurfacing, less footpath repairs and grass cutting.

"BBC Quits India" The BBC has suspended its news operations in India, as the new Indian censorship regulations are '*unacceptable*', and would prevent giving '*a fair and authentic picture of events*' there. India. Mark Tully, the correspondent, has been withdrawn.

HERE IN BRITAIN

"Chawton Festival"

The summer fete was celebrated at the village of Chawton in Hampshire, the home of Jane Austen. Schoolchildren danced round the maypole and the church where Jane's mother and sister are buried, was decorated with flowers.
Pilgrims inspected Jane's house and the oak she planted and the views she described, walking the paths she trod. She would have been moved and amused by the grand festivities with which her village is celebrating the two hundredth anniversary of her birth.

AROUND THE WORLD

"Noonday Gun Continues"

The historic noonday gun on Hong Kong's waterfront has finally been cleared of guilt in a charge of noise pollution brought by a mother in claiming that the blast frightened her child.

Her complaint caused much indignation in the Hong Kong Club and among older residents, who respect the gun as one of the colony's ancient traditions. In the words of Noel Coward's famous song "In Hong Kong they strike a gong and fire off a midday gun, but mad dogs and Englishmen go out in the noonday sun."

St Swithun's Day

St. Swithun was an Anglo-Saxon bishop of Winchester in the 9th century. Noted for humility, he was popular with the people. On his deathbed Swithin begged to be buried outside the north wall of his cathedral, unlike other religious nobility who were buried close to the altar. He wanted to be where passers-by walked, and rain fell on it. In 971 AD, the restoration and enlargement of the building was completed, and Swithin was adopted as the cathedral's patron saint. To mark the occasion, Swithun's body was dug up and re-interred on 15th July, with much ceremony, in the new cathedral behind the altar.

Numerous miracles were reported following the move. The two most famous 'miracles' are those of the Winchester egg-seller, and Queen Emma's ordeal. A woman was going to sell a basket of eggs at market. They were snatched by some workmen as a prank and got broken. In tears she prayed to St Swithun, and the eggs were 'miraculously' restored. Queen Emma, the mother of Edward the Confessor, was accused of having an affair, and to prove her innocence had to walk on red hot ploughshares. The night before her ordeal she prayed to St Swithun, and the next day was able to walk on the hot metal without injury.

According to tradition, if it rains on Saint Swithun's bridge, opposite Winchester Water Mill, on 15th July, it will rain for forty days. There is a scientific basis for this, which is that around mid-July, the jet stream settles into a pattern which holds reasonably steady until the end of August. When it lies north of Britain, continental high pressure moves in; but when it lies across or south of Britain, cooler and wetter Atlantic weather systems predominate.

August 1975

IN THE NEWS

WEEK 1   **"Rising Health Costs"** The DHSS report that the cost of prescriptions issued by doctors rose by £40m last year, with 10 million more being issued.

"Reluctant Parenting" The Office of Population Censuses and Surveys has confirmed that the trend for couples to put off having children due to the uncertain and volatile current economic situation, is likely to continue.

WEEK 2   **"Pledge to End Tied Cottages"** The Government is to abolish tied cottages on farms and give 70,000 farm workers the protection of the Rent Acts against eviction.

"Not Amused" Mary Whitehouse of the National Viewers and Listeners' Association, criticised Betty Ford, wife of the US President, for saying, *'that in general premarital relations 'with the right partner' might reduce the divorce rate'.*

WEEK 3   **"High Price of Violence"** The cost of policing fan violence outside football grounds cost the general public £750,000 last year, and may well exceed £1m this season.

"Smallpox Scare" As the World Health Organisation approaches the end of its worldwide smallpox eradication campaign, a 12-year-old British boy with suspected smallpox was admitted to a hospital in Lancashire for tests.

WEEK 4   **"Asleep at The Wheel"** A Swedish 30ft yacht was found by the Torbay lifeboat, drifting through Channel shipping lanes, with the lone crew member of the vessel sound asleep. He was sailing from the West Indies to Sweden.

"Pupil's Choice" The Scottish Council of the Labour Party's report on school truancy, suggests pupils should choose their own teachers. It stated that truants chose specific times to stay away, to avoid subjects and teachers they disliked.

HERE IN BRITAIN

"Outlook Changeable"

New BBC TV weather symbols are to be introduced to give viewers a clearer understanding after complaints that triangles (representing showers) and dots (rain) are not sufficiently intelligible.

The new system uses symbols, utilising one 'cloud', shaped like a cottage loaf, black for those threatening rain and white for others. From it will emerge blue teardrops (rain), yellow flashes (lightning) or yellow rays to illustrate that every cloud has a silver lining. Fog, however, will not have a symbol, it remains as FOG.

AROUND THE WORLD

"Kissinger Upstaged"

Elizabeth Taylor and Richard Burton arrived in Tel Aviv to make a film in Jerusalem and stole the show from the American Secretary of State, Dr Henry Kissinger.

Before they arrived at the King David I Hotel, whose historic guests have included Sir Winston Churchill and King Farouk, the star guest, Dr Kissinger, and his party had taken over the entire sixth floor. However once the Burtons were ensconced in rooms 228, 229 and 230, the talk was of nothing else!

EDINBURGH FRINGE FESTIVAL

EDINBURGH
INTERNATIONAL
FESTIVAL 24 AUGUST - 13 SEPTEMBER 1975

The population of Edinburgh almost doubled in size as visitors flocked to the capital for the annual summer Festival this month, which many would argue is the best time to visit Edinburgh as the city becomes the centre of the entertainment world. Visitors and locals alike are treated to performances in the arts, music, theatre, dance, comedy, and literature.

The Fringe started life when eight theatre companies turned up uninvited to the inaugural Edinburgh International Festival in 1947. With all the city's major venues in use, these companies took over smaller, alternative venues for their productions. It is an open access performing arts festival, meaning that there is no selection committee, and anyone may participate, with any type of performance. The official Fringe Programme categorises shows into sections for theatre, comedy, dance, theatre, circus, cabaret, children's shows, musicals, opera, music, spoken word, exhibitions, and events. Comedy is the largest section, making up over one-third of the programme, and the one that in modern times has the highest public profile.

The Edinburgh Festival has not only attracted big names like Maria Callas, Richard Burton and Donald Pleasence, but has become the springboard for many careers. Robin Williams first appeared at the Edinburgh Fringe in 1971 in a production of "The Taming of the Shrew" before going on to be a huge name on both sides of the Atlantic. Peter Cook, who became one of the leading figures in the satire boom of the 60's, first appeared here with Dudley Moore, Alan Bennet and Jonathan Miller in 'Beyond The Fringe'. The Cambridge Footlights Revue appear regularly and have introduced us to actors who have gone on to star in television and cinema such as John Cleese, and Emma Thompson.

IN THE NEWS

WEEK 1   **"Restaurant Chain in Liquidation"** 'London Eating Houses', a restaurant chain and one of the largest Wimpy bar franchisees, has stopped trading with 800 employees being made redundant.

"London Hilton Bombed" a bomb explosion at the Hilton Hotel, in the West End left two dead and 62 injured. A warning had been telephoned to a newspaper office.

WEEK 2   **"Needles for Nation"** The National Trust has bought the Needles headland, on the Isle of Wight, but the old MOD installations will need to be demolished to allow public access.

"Soviet Shadows" Russian ships shadowed the US Navy's nuclear task group arriving at Portsmouth. *"Right now, off the English Channel, the fishing fleet is not British, but Soviet. I do not think the public realise what has happened,'* the US Commander said.

WEEK 3   **"Housewives in Need"** According to the National Consumer Congress, many husbands hold onto their pay rises, while others pass on less than half for housekeeping. With rising prices, barely 20% of housewives manage.

"Pattie Hearst Arrested" The newspaper heiress, hunted by the FBI for 19 months, was arrested in San Francisco, ending the saga which began in 1974 with her kidnapping by the Symbionese Liberation Army.

WEEK 4   **"Crash Helmet Protest"** 500 Sikhs protested in Slough about a colleague's jail sentence for refusing to pay a £50 fine for twice riding his motorcycle wearing his turban instead of a crash helmet.

"Spaghetti House Siege" Gunmen representing the 'Black Liberation Front' held seven Italians hostage in a Knightsbridge restaurant after releasing one.

HERE IN BRITAIN

"Buy British"

The British motor industry has been criticised for buying car components from foreign manufacturers. There were no British locks, door handles or boot latches on any of the firm's British Leyland 18-22 models, all were being supplied by foreign firms.

In the engine, the Joseph Lucas name is on most of the electrical equipment, but at least 50% of the parts are produced in Japan or Hong Kong, using the Lucas name. 'If we want a British car, it should be a British car and not a British built car with foreign parts'.

AROUND THE WORLD

"Rembrandt Painting Slashed"

Rembrandt's painting 'The Night Watch' was slashed by a man with a bread knife who fought off a museum guard and claimed he 'did it for the Lord.' The attacker arrived shortly after the Rijksmuseum's afternoon opening, heading straight to the painting and slashing it.

The assault made over a dozen cuts, severely damaging a seven-foot section. The restoration is expected to take at least four months. This was the second knife attack on the painting in recent years.

MICHAELMAS DAY

Nottingham Goose Fair (main). A goose market (inset).

The Feast of Michael and All Angels Day, known as Michaelmas, was celebrated on the 29th September with religious ceremonies up and down the country. The day traditionally marks the beginning of Autumn and the official shortening of days, marking one of the four 'quarter days' in England. *Lady Day* in March, *Midsummer* in June, *Michaelmas* in September and *Christmas* in December make up the four 'quarter days' in traditional British folklore; spaced three months apart, the days all typically hold religious meaning and fall near an equinox or a solstice. It was on these days that servants were hired or fired, rent was collected and leases were signed. Michaelmas was originally particularly important, as it marked the end of the harvest season, but this became less so following the split from the Catholic Church under Henry VIII in the early 1530s, when the *Harvest Festival* was celebrated a few weeks later on October 10th.

Thousands of families across Britain feasted on a well fattened goose to, according to tradition, protect against financial need in the family for the next year: *'Eat a goose on Michaelmas Day, want not for money all the year.'* Because of this, Michaelmas has earned the nickname *'Goose Day'* and the famous Nottingham Goose fair is still held on the weekend closest to the festival. It stems from a rumour that goose was the food being eaten by Queen Elizabeth I upon hearing of the defeat of the Spanish Armada in 1588, vowing to finish the bird on Michaelmas in celebration.

In British folklore, Michaelmas is the last time that blackberries should be picked, as it was on this day that Lucifer was expelled from heaven, landing on a prickly blackberry bush, and proceeding to scorch it with fiery breath.

October 1975

IN THE NEWS

WEEK 1   **"Strict Labelling for Yogurt"** The Food Standards Committee wants stricter rules for labelling yoghurt. It shouldn't be called un-flavoured yoghurt just to distinguish it from yoghurt with added fruit.

"Mine Sweeping Hovercraft" A Royal Navy bomb disposal team used a hovercraft to search for and find a number of unexploded WWII bombs on the Essex marshes.

WEEK 2   **"Beefalo Bull"** The first British supplies of meat from a cow/American bison cross, called a 'beefalo', with leaner cuts and a quarter the price of beef will soon be on sale.

"Not So Sweet Tooth" Manufacturers report that Britain's sweet consumption has fallen by a tenth since last year, but that hasn't prevented the cost of sweets sold from rising by more than 25%.

WEEK 3   **"Sold Out"** Tickets for the first Concorde flights went on sale with the first three journeys fully booked. People on a register kept over the past 11 years had first choice.

"Roof Garden to Stay" The Biba store in Kensington High Street has closed after only two years of trading. However, a preservation order has been placed on the roof garden.

WEEK 4   **"Slow Down for Chrysler"** Chrysler's car assembly plant is to work only eight days in November and three days in December. The company has only worked three and four-day weeks since September.

"Rock Star Turned Sculptor" Tommy Steele has given a statue called 'Bermondsey Boy', based on and sculpted by himself, to the new Rotherhithe Civic Centre.

HERE IN BRITAIN

"Conker Championships"

64 contenders entered the 11th World Conker Championships at Ashton, in Northamptonshire. Players from around the world took part in the tournament, both teams and individuals competed in a knock-out format, with titles for men's, women's and youth categories.

The event began in 1965 when a group of anglers held a conker contest at the local pub when the weather was too bad to go fishing. A small collection was made for charity, since then the event has raised at least £2,500 for visually impaired people every year.

AROUND THE WORLD

"He is The Greatest"

Muhammad Ali retained his world heavyweight boxing title when Joe Frazier's corner stopped the fight in the 14th round in their third and final fight. The 'Thrilla in Manila' as the event was dubbed, was televised from the Philippines and streamed around the world.

Some sources estimate that the fight was watched by around 1billion people worldwide. This included 100 million viewers on closed-circuit television and 500,000 pay-per-view buys on HBO. Ali won by technical knockout (TKO) and then collapsed with exhaustion after being pronounced the winner.

TRAFALGAR DAY

Tuesday 21st October

Trafalgar Day Lunch

Join us to commemorate Nelson's famous victory

Trafalgar Day was marked in Britain this year with the traditional naval ceremony of colours aboard HMS Victory in Portsmouth. The white ensign and Union Jack were raised on the 150-year-old wooden galleon, before a flag sequence read Admiral Horatio Nelson's famous message to his fleet: *'England expects that every man will do his duty ...'.* Later, all over Britain the traditional Trafalgar Day Dinner was held, a grand affair with long-standing traditions including parading the baron of beef, Ship of the Line chocolate replica of the HMS Victory, reading of the historical dispatches, toasts and more.

Trafalgar Day is the annual celebration observed on October 21, commemorating the victory of the Royal Navy over the French and Spanish forces at the Battle of Trafalgar in 1805. The battle came at the height of the Napoleonic Wars, where France was the dominant European military power and were rapidly expanding under the leadership of Napoleon. Nevertheless, the Royal Navy proved that, under the command of Admiral Nelson, Britain still ruled the seas. On the Franco-Spanish front were 33-line ships, five frigates and two brigs, while the Royal Navy had just 27-line ships, four frigates, one schooner and one cutter. Despite being outnumbered, outflanked and hundreds of miles from the English Channel, Nelson employed ambitious tactics, capturing 18 French ships, and forcing Admiral Villeneuve to surrender. The British fleet he commanded consisted of warships built of wood, driven by sails, and equipped on both sides with cannons. After leading his fleet to one of the greatest maritime victories in history, Admiral Nelson died aboard HMS Victory after being hit by a Spanish musket ball. Nelson was fanned and brought lemonade and watered wine to drink and stayed alive until his deck commander confirmed the full surrender of French forces, three hours later.

NOVEMBER 1975

IN THE NEWS

WEEK 1 **"North Sea Oil on Stream"** The Queen pressed a button in Dyce, Aberdeen, to inaugurate the flow of North Sea oil from BP's Forties field, the largest oilfield so far discovered in the British sector and is now pumping £28 a second into the economy.

"Blast Furnace Explosion" An explosion in a 190-ton ladle of molten iron killed five and injured 14 blasting apart the 40' roof at the British Steel's complex at Scunthorpe.

WEEK 2 **"Turkey's Off"** Due to the cost, 72,000 Buckinghamshire children who stay for school lunches, will have an ordinary meal instead of the traditional Christmas fare this year.

"Speed Limits Stay" The temporary 50 mph and 60 mph speed limits on many roads, imposed last December as a fuel-saving measure, will stay in place for another year.

WEEK 3 **"Police Board Pop Music Ship"** Radio Caroline, went off the air after Essex police boarded its headquarters ship the 'Mia Amigo', in the Thames Estuary. Four men will appear in court at Southend.

"Reckless Driver" Les McKeown, the 20-year-old lead singer of the Bay City Rollers, appeared at Edinburgh Sheriff Court charged with killing an elderly woman while driving 'recklessly' in the city. *"I didn't realise I'd hit her as I didn't feel any impact,"* he said.

WEEK 4 **"Hands Up!"** Christmas supermarket shoppers were advised by an MP to hold goods they have picked up from counters, over their heads, to avoid wrongful prosecution during the 'Christmas shoplifting season'.

"You Can't Beat the Budget" The Home Office has authorised 4,000 letters to be sent out, warning that 'overlapping' colour television licences taken out to beat the April Budget increases, will be revoked.

HERE IN BRITAIN

"Women Lose Out"

The first unintended consequences of the Sex Discrimination Act emerged yesterday, as women in Liverpool lost access to cheaper train fares for shopping trips to London. British Rail had offered special 'women's day tickets', aimed at encouraging housewives to travel, with notable success.

However, British Rail lawyers have determined these offers along with phasing out women's-only waiting rooms at stations, must end to comply with the new Act, which aims to prevent gender discrimination.

AROUND THE WORLD

"Complaining Housewives"

A debate occurred between the Polish party leader, aided by the Prime Minister and several hundred Communist Party women, who complained about the hardships faced by housewives in Poland. The televised discussion focused on the shortage and poor quality of consumer goods.

Both officials acknowledged the country's economic and housing challenges, admitting many products were substandard suggesting it would be 'ideal if each worker desired to buy the products they produced.'

STIR UP SUNDAY

'Stir-up Sunday' is a centuries old tradition, where on the last Sunday before Advent, housewives start 'stirring up' their Christmas puddings. It is a family affair, and even children are allowed to help weigh out and mix all the ingredients ready for steaming the pudding. Everyone is expected to take a turn to stir the pudding mix, for each person can make a special wish for the year ahead. Traditionally, the pudding should be stirred from east to west, in honour of the Wise Men who travelled from the East to visit the baby Jesus.

Rich Christmas puddings and fruit cakes benefit from being made this much in advance because it allows the flavours to intensify, and the colour deepen over time. Puddings can be re-steamed each week and many people will also 'feed' their cakes by pricking the base and pouring an eggcup full of brandy or rum over it, before wrapping it up again carefully to preserve the moisture. By Christmas, a good cake or pudding will be 'black and rotten' – very rich indeed!

The Christmas pudding originated in the 14th-century as a sort of porridge, originally known as 'frumenty', which bore little resemblance to the pudding we know today but, in the 17th century, changes to the recipe were made. It was thickened with eggs, breadcrumbs, dried fruit and beer or spirits were added – and it came to resemble something a bit more like a sweet pudding. Nowadays, the ingredients include raisins, currants, suet, brown sugar, breadcrumbs, carrot, mixed peel, flour, mixed spices, eggs, milk and brandy, which are all essential for keeping qualities. Puddings were traditionally boiled in a 'pudding cloth', although today are usually steamed in a basin, then brought to the table with a sprig of holly, doused in brandy and set alight.

DECEMBER 1975

IN THE NEWS

WEEK 1　　**"Kirby Disaster Area"** Merseyside police have called for investment in Kirkby, blaming government neglect and inadequate infrastructure for economic decline and crime there, despite good local support.

"107 Schools Go Independent" At least 107 of the 173 direct-grant grammar schools in England and Wales have decided to become independent rather than comprehensive.

WEEK 2　　**"Christmas Cheese Ceremony"** The Christmas Cheese ceremony of 1692, took place at the Royal Hospital, in Chelsea, where a large wheel of cheese was blessed, before being cut with a sword, by one of the pensioners.

"Fog Affects Flights and Roads" Ice and dense fog seriously disrupted both road and air journeys, with visibility as low as one yard in Kent.

WEEK 3　　**"First Female QC"** Judge Patricia Coles has become the first woman of Lincoln's Inn to be made a QC after being sworn in as circuit judge by the Lord Chancellor.

"Smelly Dispute" 21 workers at the Liverpool Leyland Triumph car plant went on strike complaining about the smell from stray cats. 600 men stopped work while cleaners spent 45 minutes scrubbing the floor, whereupon the men protested that the floor was too wet and dangerous to work on.

WEEK 4　　**"All at Sea"** Light-keeper Donald McLeod said goodbye to his family in Stromness, Orkney, to spend a month on Sule Skerry, 30 miles west of Orkney in the Atlantic, Britain's most distant lighthouse.

"Salvation Army" Up to 2,200 of London's down-and-outs enjoyed some Christmas cheer at Salvation Army hostels with free meals, including turkey with all the trimmings.

HERE IN BRITAIN

"Laddo The Lion"

Laddo's owner is ready to defy a West Midland's court ruling forbidding him to keep a lion at his home in Cradley Heath. He appeared in court with a lion tamer, who lives at the same address. They were charged with behaving in a manner likely to cause a breach of the peace, by taking a wild animal for a tour around Birmingham.

The case was adjourned for nine days. The accused commented, *"I am taking my lion out and I do not care if I get arrested and put in jail. He needs exercise badly."*

AROUND THE WORLD

"Fiji Island Paradise"

The American Theatre Film Corporation of Los Angeles wanted to film a thrilling event similar to that described in Peter Benchley's novel 'Jaws' and they chose the tropical island of Fiji for the location. The event was to be a fight to the death between an experienced Australian diver and a 17' killer shark.

However, the fight, which would have netted the diver a fee of $1m, has been banned by the Fiji Government, as they objected to their island paradise being made the site for a blood sport.

THE TRAFALGAR TREE

Norway's annual gift of a Christmas tree is in pride of place at Trafalgar Square, although the original excitement over the tree and its lights has somewhat dimmed over the years. The Acton Gazette led with the spartan headline, *'The traditional lighting-up of the Trafalgar Square Christmas tree is taking place tomorrow,'* and one gentleman due to retire commented, *'Tree? Who cares?'*

The first tree was sent from Oslo in 1947 as a token of gratitude to the British people for their help during the second world war when Great Britain was Norway's closest ally. London was where the Norwegian King Haakon VII and his government fled as their country was occupied, and it was from here that much of Norway's resistance movement was organised. Both the BBC and its Norwegian counterpart NRK would broadcast in Norwegian from London, something that was both an important source of information and a boost of morale for those who remained in Norway, where people would listen in secret to their forbidden radios. The idea to send a pine to Britain was first conceived by the Norwegian naval commando, Mons Urangsvå, who sent a tree from the island of Hisøy which had been cut down during a raid to London in 1942 as a gift to King Haakon and King George V decided that it should be installed in Trafalgar Square where it stood *'evergreen with defiant hope'*.

The trees come from the snow-covered forest area surrounding Oslo, known as "Oslomarka", an area populated with moose, lynx, roe deer, and even the odd wolf, and legions of pine trees. A worthy tree is located by the head forester and space is cleared around it to allow light from all angles, and it is tended through the years to secure optimal growth.

1970 - 1974

1970:

Jan: The age of majority for most legal purposes was reduced from 21 to 18 under terms of the Family Law Reform Act 1969.

Mar: Ian Smith declares Rhodesia a Republic and the British government refuses to recognise the new state.

1971:

Feb: Decimal Day. The UK and the Republic of Ireland both change to decimal currency.

Mar: The 'Daily Sketch', Britain's oldest tabloid newspaper is absorbed by the 'Daily Mail' after 62 years.

1972:

June: The 'Watergate' scandal begins in Richard Nixon's administration in the US.

Sep: The school leaving age in the UK was raised from 15 to 16 for pupils leaving at the end of the academic year.

1973:

Jan: The United Kingdom joins the European Economic Community, later to become the EU.

Sep: The IRA detonate bombs in Manchester and Victoria Station London and two days later, Oxford St. and Sloane Square.

1974:

Jan: Until March, the 3-day week is introduced by the Conservative Government to conserve electricity during the miners' strike.

Nov: 21 people are killed and 182 injured when the IRA set bombs in two Birmingham pubs.

1974: McDonald's open their first UK restaurant in South London. The traditional café was losing out, slow ordering and service with food served at tables was not as appealing as the clean, fast service and lower prices of this new fast food.

1974: In February, Harold Wilson becomes Prime Minister for the second time (first 1964-70) with a minority Government after Edward Heath resigns having failed to clinch a coalition with the Liberals. In the second general election of the year in October, Labour win with a majority of only 3 seats.

1975 - 1979

In June and July 1976, the UK experienced a heat wave. Temperatures peak at 35.9° and the whole country suffers a severe drought. Forest fires broke out, crops failed, and reservoirs dried up causing serious water shortages. The heatwave also produced swarms of ladybirds across the south and east.

On the 7th June,1977, more than one million people lined the streets of London to watch the Queen and Prince Phillip lead a procession in the golden state coach, to St Paul's at the start of a week of the Queen's Silver Jubilee celebrations – 25 years on the throne. People all over the country held street or village parties to celebrate, more than 100,000 cards were received by the Queen and 30,000 Jubilee medals were given out.

1975:
Feb: Margaret Thatcher defeats Edward Heath to become the first female leader of the Conservative Party.

Apr: The Vietnam War ends with the Fall of Saigon to the Communists. South Vietnam surrenders unconditionally.

1976:
Mar: Harold Wilson announces his resignation as Prime Minister and James Callaghan is elected to the position in April.

Oct: The Intercity 125 high speed passenger train is introduced. Initially Paddington to Bristol and south Wales.

1977:
Jan: Jimmy Carter is sworn in as the 39th President of the United States, succeeding Gerald Ford.

Sep: Freddie Laker launches his 'Skytrain' with a single fare, Gatwick to New York, at £59 compared to £189.

1978:
Aug: Louise Brown becomes the world's first human born 'in vitro fertilisation' – test tube baby.

Nov: An industrial dispute shuts down The Times newspaper – until November 1979.

1979:
Mar: Airey Neave, politician and WW2 veteran, is blown up in the House of Commons carpark by the Irish National Liberation Army.

May: Margaret Thatcher becomes the first female Prime Minister of the United Kingdom. The Conservatives win a 43 seat majority.

THE HOME

Increasing Comfort and Prosperity

Homes became brighter and more comfortable in the 1970's. Teenagers could lie on the 'impossible to clean', loopy shag pile carpet watching films on VHS video cassettes or watch live programmes on the family's colour television set.

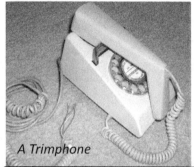

A Trimphone

The ubiquitous macramé owl, or plant holder complete with trailing spider plant, might dangle in the corner adjacent to the bulky, stone faced, rustic fireplace. Bathroom suites were often Avocado green and 'downstairs loos' were a statement of the houseowners ideals! If you were one of the 35% of households in Britain to own a telephone, you could catch up with friends and family on the new 'warbling' Trimphone, maybe sitting on your bright, floral covered couch.

Labour Saving Devices

The previous decade had been prosperous and the advances in technology continued such that by the 1970s, most households had many labour-saving devices. Sales of freezers rose rapidly in the 70s and by 1974, one in ten households had a freezer - mainly full of peas, chips and fish fingers but also ice cream, previously a rare treat, and in large quantities. Bulk buying food meant less time shopping and the Magimix food processor which added a choice of blades and attachments to a standard liquidiser, made home cooking more adventurous.

Teenage Home Entertainment

Teenagers covered their bedroom walls with posters of their favourite bands and actors, ranging from Rod Stewart and the Boomtown Rats to Olivia Newton-John and Robert Redford. The lucky ones listening to top ten singles on their own stereo record deck which had replaced the old Dansette player.

If they wanted to play the new video games, they typically went to an arcade, but in 1975, Atari PONG was released, the first commercially successful video game you could play at home on your television. Based on a simple two-dimensional graphical representation of a tennis-like game, two players used paddles to hit a ball back and forth on a black and white screen. It captivated audiences and its success influenced developers to invent more and increasingly sophisticated games for the home market.

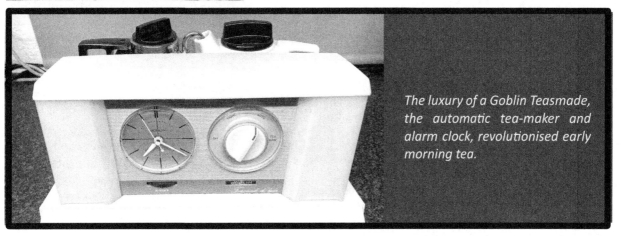

The luxury of a Goblin Teasmade, the automatic tea-maker and alarm clock, revolutionised early morning tea.

ART AND CULTURE

1970 - 1974

1970 Laurence Olivier becomes the first actor to be made a Lord. He is given a life peerage in the Queen's Birthday Honours list.
The first Glastonbury Festival was held, called the Worthy Farm Pop Festival. About 1500 attended.

1971 Coco Chanel, the French fashion designer died. (Born 1883)
The 'Blue Peter' presenters buried a time capsule in the grounds of BBC Television Centre, due to be opened on the first episode in 2000.
Mr Tickle, the first of the Mr Men books is published.

1972 'Jesus Christ Superstar', the Tim Rice & Andrew Lloyd Webber musical opens in the West End.
John Betjeman is appointed Poet Laureate.

1973 The British Library is established by merger of the British Museum Library & the National Lending Library for Science & Technology.
Series 1 of the BBC sitcom, 'Last of the Summer Wine' begins. There are eventually, 31 series.

1974 'Tinker, Tailor, Soldier, Spy' the first of John Le Carré's novel featuring the ageing spymaster, George Smiley, is published.
The Terracotta Army of Qin Shi Huang, thousands of life-size clay models of soldiers, horses and chariots, is discovered at Xi'an in China.

Milton Keynes Shopping Centre

1975 - 1979

1975 Donald Coggan is enthroned as the Archbishop of Canterbury.
Bill Gates and Paul Allen found Microsoft in Albuquerque, New Mexico.

1976 Trevor Nunn's memorable production of 'Macbeth' opens at Stratford-upon-Avon, with Ian McKellan and Judi Dench in the lead roles.
The Royal National Theatre on the South Bank opens.
Agatha Christie's last novel, Sleeping Murder, a Miss Marple story is published posthumously.

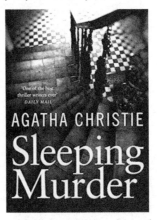

1977 Luciano Pavarotti makes his television debut singing in Puccini's La Boheme in the television debut of 'Live from the Met'.
Mike Leigh's satire on the aspirations and tastes of the new middle class emerging in the 70's, 'Abigail's Party', opened at the Hampstead Theatre starring Alison Steadman.

1978 The Andrew Lloyd Webber musical 'Evita' opens in London.
The arcade video game, 'Space Invaders' is released.

1979 Margaret Thatcher opens the new Central Milton Keynes Shopping Centre, the largest indoor shopping centre in Britain.
Anthony Blunt, British art historian and former Surveyor of the Queen's Pictures, in exposed as a double agent for the Soviets during WW2.
The Sony Walkman, portable cassette player is released.

In The 1970s

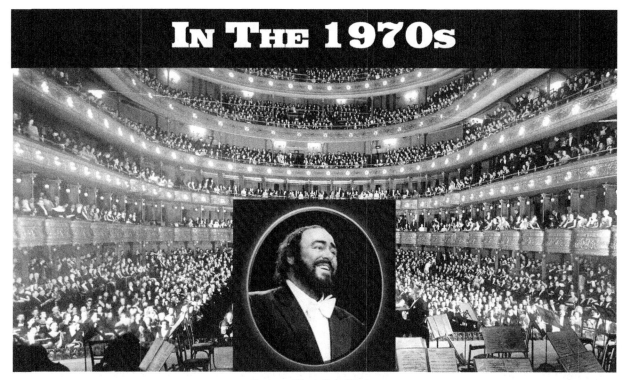

Pavarotti at the Met.

It was in his third season at the Metropolitan Opera House in New York that Luciano Pavarotti, the operatic tenor, would skyrocket to stardom. The company imported Covent Garden's production of Donizetti's *La Fille du Régiment* in 1972 as a vehicle for Joan Sutherland. The great Australian diva enjoyed a huge triumph, but the surprise for the audience was the young Italian tenor by her side who shared an equal part in the phenomenal success. This was the historic first Met performance telecast live on PBS as part of the long-running series that continues to the present day.

The Terracotta Army

'The Qin Tomb Terracotta Warriors and Horses' was constructed between 246-206BC as an afterlife guard for China's First Emperor, Qin Shihuang, from whom, China gets its name. He ordered it built to remember the army he led to triumph over other warring states, and to unite China.

The tomb and the army were all made by hand by some 700,000 artisans and labourers, and comprises thousands of life-size soldiers, each with different facial features and expressions, clothing, hairstyles and gestures, arranged in battle array.

All figures face east, towards the ancient enemies of Qin State, in rectangular formations and three separate vaults include rows of kneeling and standing archers, chariot war configurations and mixed forces of infantry, horse drawn chariots plus numerous soldiers armed with long spears, daggers and halberds.

FILMS

1970 - 1974

1970 Love Story, was the biggest grossing film a sentimental, tearjerker with the oft-quoted tagline, "Love means never having to say you're sorry." Nominated for the Academy Awards Best Picture, it was beaten by **Patton** which won 7 major titles that year.

1971 The Oscar winner was **The French Connection** with Gene Hackman as a New York police detective, Jimmy 'Popeye' Doyle, chasing down drug smugglers. Hackman was at the peak of his career in the 70's.

1972 Francis Ford Coppola's gangster saga, **The Godfather** became the highest grossing film of its time and helped drive a resurgence in the American film industry.

1973 Glenda Jackson won Best Actress for her role in **A Touch of Class.** She revealed that she was approached for the part by the director after appearing in the 1971 'Antony & Cleopatra' sketch on the Morecambe & Wise show. After she won, Eric Morecambe sent her a telegram saying, "Stick with us and we will get you another one".

1974 New films this year included **The Godfather Part II,** which won the Oscar, **Blazing Saddles** the comedy western and the disaster film, **The Towering Inferno** starring Paul Newman and Steve McQueen.

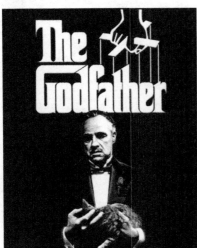

1975 - 1979

1975 One Flew Over the Cuckoo's Nest, an allegorical film set in a mental hospital, starring Jack Nicholson, beat tough competition for Best Picture from Spielberg's **Jaws** and Altman's **Nashville.**

1976 Jodi Foster won an Oscar in Martin Scorsese's gritty film **Taxi Driver** which examines alienation in urban society but it was Sylvester Stallone's **Rocky** that carried off the Best Picture award.

1977 Annie Hall from Woody Allen, the winner of Best Picture is a masterpiece of witty and quotable one-liners.

1978 The Vietnam War is examined through the lives of three friends from a small steel-mill town before, during and after their service in **The Deer Hunter**. A powerful and disturbing film.

1979 In this year's Best Picture, **Kramer v Kramer** there is a restaurant scene where Dustin Hoffman throws his wine glass at the wall. Only the cameraman was forewarned, Meryl Streep's shocked reaction was genuine!

IN THE 1970s

Star Wars

Star Wars all began with George Lucas's eponymous film in 1977. The epic space fantasy, telling the adventures of characters "A long time ago in a galaxy far, far away", and this first film was a world beater in special effects technology using new computerised and digital effects. It rapidly became a phenomenon, Luke Skywalker, Jedi Knights, Princess Leia and Darth Vader becoming household names. An immensely valuable franchise grew up to include the films, television series, video games, books, comics and theme parks which now amounts to billions of dollars and the film introduced the phrase "May the Force be with you" into common usage.

TWENTIETH CENTURY-FOX Presents A LUCASFILM LTD PRODUCTION STAR WARS
Starring MARK HAMILL HARRISON FORD CARRIE FISHER
PETER CUSHING
and
ALEC GUINNESS
Written and Directed by   Produced by   Music by
GEORGE LUCAS   GARY KURTZ   JOHN WILLIAMS
PANAVISION® PRINTS BY DE LUXE® TECHNICOLOR®
Making Films Sound Better
DOLBY SYSTEM
Noise Reduction · High Fidelity

Apocalypse Now

Joseph Conrad's book 'Heart of Darkness' was the inspiration for producer and director Francis Ford Coppola's psychological film, a metaphor for the madness and folly of war itself for a generation of young American men. Beautiful, with symbolic shots showing the confusion, violence and fear of the nightmare of the Vietnam War, much of it was filmed on location in the Philippines where expensive sets were destroyed by severe weather, a typhoon called 'Olga', Marlon Brando showed up on set overweight and completely unprepared and Martin Sheen had a near-fatal heart attack.

This led to the film being two and a half times over budget and taking twice the number of scheduled weeks to shoot. When filming finally finished, the release was postponed several times as Coppola had six hours of film to edit. The helicopter attack scene with the 'Ride of the Valkyries' soundtrack is one of the most memorable film scenes ever.

Women Wear the Trousers

It is often said that 1970s styles had no direction and were too prolific. French couture no longer handed down diktats of what we should be wearing, and the emerging street style was inventive, comfortable, practical for women or glamorous. It could be home-made, it was whatever you wanted it to be, and the big new trend was for gender neutral clothes, women wore trousers in every walk of life, trouser suits for the office, jeans at home and colourful, tight-fitting ones for in between. Trouser legs became wider and 'bell-bottoms', flared from the knee down, with bottom leg openings of up to twenty-six inches, made from denim, bright cotton and satin polyester, became mainstream. Increasingly 'low cut', they were teamed with platform soles or high cut boots until they could not flare anymore, and so, by the end of the decade they had gone, skin-tight trousers, in earth tones, greys, whites and blacks were much more in vogue.

And the Hot Pants

In the early 70s, women's styles were very flamboyant with extremely bright colours and, in the winter, long, flowing skirts and trousers *but* come the summer, come the Hot Pants. These extremely short shorts were made of luxury fabrics such as velvet and satin designed for fashionable wear, not the practical equivalents for sports or leisure, and they enjoyed great popularity until falling out of fashion in the middle of the decade. Teamed with skin-tight t-shirts, they were favourites for clubwear and principally worn by women, including Jacqueline Kennedy Onassis, Elizabeth Taylor and Jane Fonda, but they were also worn by some high-profile men, David Bowie, Sammy Davis Jnr and Liberace among them, although the shorts were slightly longer than the women's versions, but still shorter than usual. Chest hair, medallions, sideburns and strangely, tennis headbands, finished the look!

These Boots Are Made For Walking

Boots were so popular in the early 1970s that even men were getting in on the action. It wasn't uncommon to see a man sporting 2" inch platform boots inspired by John Travolta in Saturday Night Fever. The trend was all about being sexy on the dance floor!

And Punk Was Not to Be Ignored

Emerging in the mid 70s in London as an anarchic and aggressive movement, a few hundred young people defined themselves as an anti-fashion urban youth street culture closely aligned to the music that became punk. They cut up old clothes from charity shops, destroyed the fabric and refashioned outfits in a manner intended to shock. Trousers were deliberately torn to reveal laddered tights and dirty legs and worn with heavy Doc Martens footwear, now seen on many young women too.

Safety pins and chains held bits of fabric together. Neck chains were made from padlocks and chain and even razor blades were used as pendants. Body piercings and studs, beginning with the three-stud earlobe, progressing to the ear outline embedded with ear studs, evolved to pins in eyebrows, cheeks, noses or lips and together with tattoos were the beginning of unisex fashion. All employed by male and female alike to offend. Vivienne Westwood and Malcolm McLaren quickened the style with her bondage shop "Sex", and his punk music group, the "Sex Pistols".

Saturday Morning TV

In the early 70s, Saturday mornings for many children still meant a trip to the cinema but with the advent of Saturday Morning Television, under instruction 'not to wake their parents', children could creep downstairs, switch on the box and stay entertained until lunchtime.

First, in 1974, came ITV's 'Tiswas', hosted by Chris Tarrant it was a chaotic blend of jokes, custard pies and buckets of water.

Then in 1976, the BBC introduced 'Swap Shop' with Noel Edmonds, Keith Chegwin and John Craven and a Saturday morning ritual was born. Nearly three hours of ground-breaking television using the 'phone-in' extensively for the first time on TV. The programme included music, competitions, cartoons and spontaneous nonsense from Edmonds. There was coverage of news and issues relevant to children, presented by 'Newsround's' John Craven but by far the most popular element of the show was the "Swaporama" open-air event, hosted by Chegwin. An outside broadcast unit would travel to different locations throughout the UK where sometimes as many as 2000 children would gather to swap their belongings with others.

Saturday Night Fever

Memories of Saturday night and Sunday morning in the discotheque. A mirror ball; strobe lights; 'four on the floor' rhythm; the throb of the bass drum; girls in Spandex tops with hot pants or vividly coloured, shiny, Lycra trousers with equally dazzling halter neck tops; boys in imitations of John Travolta's white suit from Saturday Night Fever risking life and limb on towering platform shoes.

These glamorous dancers, clad in glitter, metallic lame and sequins, gyrating as the music pounded out at the direction of the DJ, whirling energetically and glowing bright 'blue-white' under the ultra-violet lights as their owners 'strutted their stuff', perspiration running in rivulets down their backs.

The DJs, stars in their own right, mixed tracks by Donna Summer, the Bee Gees, Gloria Gaynor, Sister Sledge, Chic and Chaka Khan, as their sexy followers, fuelled by the night club culture of alcohol and drugs, changed from dancing the Hustle with their partners to the solo freestyle dancing of John Travolta.

In The 1970s

The Dangers of Leisure

In the 1970's the Government was intent on keeping us all – and particularly children – safe and continued producing the wartime Public Information Films, which were still scaring children witless!

1971: Children and Disused Fridges: Graphic warnings of children being suffocated in old fridges that, tempted by their playful imaginations, they want to climb into.

1973: Broken Glass: This film shows a boy running on the sand, ending abruptly before he steps on a broken glass bottle, the film urges people to use a bin or take their litter home with them.

1974: The Fatal Floor: This 30 second film had the message, "Polish a floor, put a rug on it, and you might as well set a man trap…"

1979: Play Safe – Frisbee: This film used chilling electronic music and frightening sound effects to highlight the potentially fatal combination of frisbees with electricity pylons and kites, fishing rods and radio-controlled planes.

1972: Teenagers – Learn to Swim:

A cartoon aimed at teenagers warns them to learn how to swim, or risk social embarrassment and failure to attract the opposite sex. The female character's illusion of her boyfriend 'Dave' being able 'to do anything' is shattered after she wishes they were at the seaside, where she discovers Dave can't swim. He in turn wishes he didn't 'keep losing me birds' after his girlfriend disappears with 'Mike' who 'swims like a fish'. Although the film is light-hearted in tone it was intended in part to help prevent accidents.

1975: Protect and Survive:

This was the title of a series of booklets and films made in the late 1970s and early 1980s, dealing with emergency planning for a nuclear war including the recognition of attack warning, fallout warning, and all-clear signals, the preparation of a home "fallout room" and the stockpiling of food, water, and other emergency supplies. In the opinion of some contemporary critics, the films *were deeply and surprisingly fatalistic in tone*!

MUSIC

1970 - 1974

1970 Number 1 for 3 weeks, **Bridge Over Troubled Water** by Simon and Garfunkel became their 'signature song' selling over 6m copies worldwide. It also became one of the most performed songs of the 20th century, covered by over 50 artists.

1971 George Harrison's first release as a solo **My Sweet Lord** topped the charts for five weeks and became the best selling UK single of the year.
Rod Stewart had 7 No 1's this year including in October, the double sided hits, **Reason to Believe/Maggie May**

1972 A jingle, rewritten to become the hugely popular 'Buy the world a Coke' advert for the Coca Cola company, was re-recorded by The New Seekers as the full-length song, **I'd Like to Teach the World to Sing**, which stayed at No 1 for 4 weeks.

1973 Dawn featuring Tony Orlando had the bestselling single of 1973 with **"Tie a Yellow Ribbon Round the 'Ole Oak Tree"**, which spent four weeks at the top spot and lasted 11 weeks in the top ten.
Queen released their debut album, **"Queen"**. The Carpenters reached number 2 with **"Yesterday Once More"**.

1974 **Waterloo**, the winning song for Sweden in the Eurovision Song Contest began ABBA's journey to world-wide fame.
David Essex has his first No 1 with **Wanna Make You a Star** which spends 3 weeks at the top of the charts.

1975 - 1979

1975 **Make Me Smile** (Come Up and See Me) was a chart topper for Steve Harley & Cockney Rebel. **Bohemian Rhapsody** for Queen, stayed at the top for nine weeks.

1976 The Brotherhood of Man won the Eurovision Song Contest for Great Britain with **Save Your Kisses for Me**. It became the biggest-selling song of the year and remains one of the biggest-selling Eurovision winners ever.
Don't Go Breaking My Heart was the first No. 1 single in the UK for both Elton John and Kiki Dee.

1977 Actor David Soul, riding high on his success in Starsky & Hutch, had the No 1 spot for 4 weeks with **Don't Give Up on Us**.
Way Down was the last song to be recorded by Elvis Presley before his death and stayed at No 1 for 5 weeks.

1978 Kate Bush released her debut single, **Wuthering Heights,** which she had written aged 18 after watching Emily Brontë's Wuthering Heights on television and discovering she shared the author's birthday.
Spending five weeks at the top of the British charts, Boney M's **"Rivers of Babylon"** became the biggest selling single of the year, exceeding one million sales between May and June.

1979 Frequently recalled as a symbol of female empowerment, **I Will Surviv**e reached the top for Gloria Gaynor.
The Wall, Pink Floyd's rock opera was released, featuring all three parts of **Another Brick in the Wall. Part 2**, written as a protest against rigid schooling was No1 in Dec.

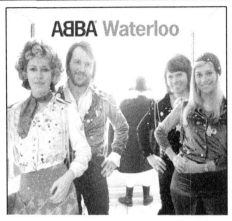

ABBA Waterloo

The Decade in Numbers

Most No1 Singles:
ABBA with seven.
Waterloo (1974);
Mamma Mia, Fernando
and
Dancing Queen (all 1976);
Knowing Me Knowing You,
The Name of the Game,
(both 1977);
Take a Chance on Me
(1978).

Most Weeks at No 1:
Bohemian Rhapsody by
Queen; **Mull of Kintyre /**
Girl's School by Wings;
You're the One That I Want
by John Travolta and Olivia
Newton-John.

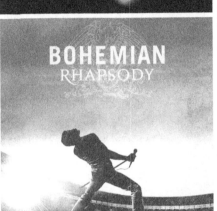

BOHEMIAN
RHAPSODY

WINGS

MULL OF KINTYRE

'Danny' and 'Sandy' Fever

Grease, the 1978 musical romantic comedy starring John
Travolta (Danny) and Olivia Newton-John (Sandy) had
phenomenal success. In June to August 1978, **You're the**
One That I Want and in September to October, **Summer**
Nights, locked up the number 1 position for a total of
sixteen weeks.

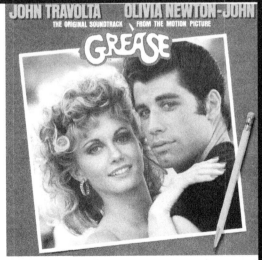

JOHN TRAVOLTA   OLIVIA NEWTON-JOHN
THE ORIGINAL SOUNDTRACK   FROM THE MOTION PICTURE
GREASE

Hopelessly Devoted to You was nominated for an
Oscar and John Travolta and Olivia Newton-John
seemed to be constantly in the public conscience.
Critically and commercially successful, the soundtrack
album ended 1978 as the second best -selling album in
the US, behind the soundtrack of the 1977 blockbuster
Saturday Night Fever, which also starred John
Travolta.

Pocket Calculators

The first pocket calculators came onto the market towards the end of 1970. In the early 70s they were an expensive status symbol but by the middle of the decade, businessmen were quite used to working their sales figures out quickly whilst 'out of the office'.

Household accounts were made easy and children wished they could use them at school – not just to help with homework. Most early calculators performed only basic addition, subtraction, multiplication and division but the speed and accuracy, sometimes giving up to 12 digit answers, of the machine proved sensational.

In 1972, Hewlett Packard introduced the revolutionary HP-35 pocket calculator which, in addition to the basic operations, enabled advanced mathematical functions. It was the first scientific, hand-held calculator, able to perform a wide number of logarithmic and trigonometric functions, store intermediate solutions and utilise scientific notations.

With intense competition, prices of pocket calculators dropped rapidly, and the race was on to produce the smallest possible models. The target was to be no bigger than a credit card. Casio won the race.

The Miracle of IVF

In 1971, Patrick Steptoe, gynaecologist, Robert Edwards, biologist, and Jean Purdy, nurse and embryologist set up a small laboratory at the Kershaw's Hospice in Oldham which was to lead to the development of in vitro fertilisation and eventual birth of Louise Brown in 1978.

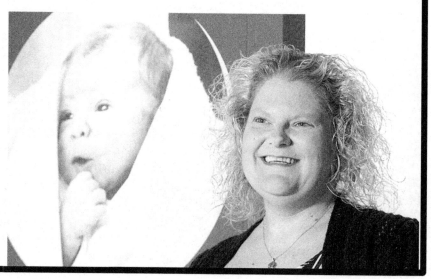

They developed a technique for retrieving eggs at the right time and fertilising them in the laboratory, believing that they could be implanted back in the uterus. It took more than 80 embryo transfers before the first successful pregnancy, and the birth of Louise, the first 'test-tube baby', heralded the potential happiness of infertile people and a bright future for British science and industry.

IN THE 1970s

"Houston We Have a Problem"

In April 1970, two days after the launch of Apollo 13, the seventh crewed mission in the Apollo space program and the third meant to land on the Moon, the NASA ground crew heard the now famous message, "Houston, we've had a problem." An oxygen tank had exploded, and the lunar landing was aborted leaving the astronauts in serious danger. The crew looped around the Moon and returned safely to Earth, their safe return being down to the ingenuity under pressure by the crew, commanded by Jim Lovell, together with the flight controllers and mission control. The crew experienced great hardship, caused by limited power, a chilly and wet cabin and a shortage of drinking water.

Even so, Apollo 13 set a spaceflight record for the furthest humans have travelled from Earth.

Tens of millions of viewers watched Apollo 13 splashdown in the South Pacific Ocean and the recovery by USS Iwo Jima.

The global campaigning network **Greenpeace** was founded in 1971 by Irving and Dorothy Stowe, environmental activists. The network now has 26 independent national or regional organisations in 55 countries worldwide.

Their stated goal is to ensure the ability of the earth to nurture life in all its diversity. To achieve this they "use non-violent, creative confrontation to expose global environmental problems, and develop solutions for a green and peaceful future". In detail to:

- Stop the planet from warming beyond 1.5° in order to prevent the most catastrophic impacts of the climate breakdown.
- Protect biodiversity in all its forms.
- Slow the volume of hyper-consumption and learn to live within our means.
- Promote renewable energy as a solution that can power the world.
- Nurture peace, global disarmament and non-violence.

SPORT

1970 - 1974

1970 The thoroughbred 'Nijinsky', wins all three English Triple Crown Races: **The 2,000 Guineas** at Newmarket; **The Derby** at Epsom; the **St. Leger Stakes** at Doncaster and the Irish Derby. The first horse to do this in 35 years and not repeated as of 2021.

1971 Arsenal wins both the **First Division** title and the **FA Cup**, becoming the fourth team ever to win the double.
Jack Nicklaus wins his ninth major at the **PGA Championship**, the first golfer ever to win all four majors for the second time.

1972 At **Wimbledon**, Stan Smith (US) beat Ilie Nastase in the Men's Singles Final. It was his only Wimbledon title.
In the Women's Final, Billie Jean King (US) beat Yvonne Goolagong (AUS) to gain her fourth **Wimbledon** title.
The **Olympic Games** held in Munich are overshadowed by the murder of eleven Israeli athletes and coaches by Palestinian Black September members.

1973 George Foreman knocks out Joe Frazier in only two rounds to take the **World Heavyweight Boxing** Championship title.

Red Rum wins the **Grand National** with a new record and staging a spectacular comeback on the run-in having trailed the leader by 15 lengths at the final fence.

1974 Liverpool win the **FA Cup Final** against Newcastle United at Wembley. Kevin Keegan scored two of their three goals.
Eddie Merckx wins the **Tour de France**, becoming the first rider to win the Triple Crown of Cycling, **Tour de France**, **Giro d'Italia** and **World Championships** in one calendar year.

1975 - 1979

1975 In athletics, John Walker (NZ) sets a new world record becoming the first man to **run a mile** in under 3 mins 50 seconds. He clocks 3mins 49.4 secs.
Muhammad Ali defeats Joe Frazier in the 'Thrilla In Manilla' to maintain the **Boxing Heavyweight Championship** of the world.

1976 The **Olympics** are held in Montreal. Britain's only medal is a Bronze, won by Brendan Foster running the **10,000 metres**.
John Curry, becomes the **European, Olympic and World Figure Skating Champion**. He was the first skater to combine, ballet and modern dance into his skating.

1977 The commercial **World Series Cricket** was introduced by Kerry Packer. WSC changed the nature of the game with its emphasis on the "gladiatorial" aspect of fast bowling and heavy promotion of fast bowlers.

1978 During the **Oxford and Cambridge Boat Race,** the Cambridge boat sinks. It is the first sinking in the race since 1951.
Wales wins the rugby **Five Nations Championship** and completes the Grand Slam having beaten England, France, Ireland and Scotland.

1978 Arsenal beat Manchester United 3-2 in the **FA Cup Final.**
At **The Open** at Royal Lytham & St Annes Golf Club Seve Ballesteros becomes the first golfer from Continental Europe to win a major since 1907.

Traffic Lights and Football

Before the introduction of Red and Yellow Cards in football, cautions or sending a player off had to be dealt with orally, and the language barrier could sometimes present problems. For example, in the 1966 World Cup, the German referee tried in vain to send Argentinian player Antonio Rattin off the field, but Rattin did not 'want' to understand and eventually was escorted off the pitch by the police! Ken Aston, Head of World Cup Referees, was tasked with solving this problem and legend has it that the idea of the red and yellow cards came to him when he was stopped in his car at traffic lights. They were tested in the 1968 Olympics and the 1970 World Cup in Mexico and introduced to European leagues soon after and after six years, to English football.

In 1976, the first player to be sent off using a red card in an English game was Blackburn Rovers winger David Wagstaffe.

Tour de France

In 1974 the Tour de France covered 2,546 miles in 22 stages, one of which was the first to be held in the UK, a circuit stage on the Plympton By-pass near Plymouth. Eddy Merckx of Belgium won eight stages and won the race overall with a comfortable margin, making it five wins for him out of his five Tours. He also won that year's Combination Classification – the General (Yellow Jersey), Points or Sprint (Green Jersey) and Mountains (since 1975, King of the Mountains wears the Polka Dot Jersey).

Rockstar and Racing Driver

James Hunt, the charismatic, play-boy darling of the press in the 1970's, began his Formula 1 career at the beginning of the decade with the Hesketh Racing team and gave them their only win in 1975 at the Dutch GP. He moved to McLaren in 1976, and in his first year with them, he and his great rival Niki Lauda at Ferrari, fought an epic season-long battle. It was an extraordinarily dramatic season, over sixteen races filled with drama and controversy, where Lauda had gained an early championship lead. By the final race in Japan, he was being reeled-in by Hunt and was only three points ahead. Hunt drove the race of his life, in the worst possible weather conditions, to finish in third place. Lauda, already badly injured from the crash at Nürburgring in August, withdrew because of the hazardous conditions which meant James Hunt became World Champion, winning by just a single point.

Hunt's natural driving ability was phenomenal, and while his habit of risk-taking didn't always endear him to others, hence the nickname "Hunt the Shunt", it also made him compelling to watch. Off track, he and Niki had an enduring friendship, which lasted after James's retirement from F1 in 1979 until his untimely death from a heart attack in 1993, aged just 45.

TRANSPORT

ICONIC MACHINES OF THE DECADE

The Jumbo Jet
Entered service on January 22, 1970. The 747 was the first airplane dubbed a "Jumbo Jet", the first wide-body airliner.

In 1971 Ford launched the car that was to represent the 1970s, the Cortina Mk III. In 1976 the Mk IV and 1979 Mk V. Cortinas were the best-selling cars of the decade.

The best-selling foreign import was the Datsun Sunny, which was only the 19th best-selling car of the decade.

In 1973, British Leyland's round, dumpy shaped Allegro was not at all popular and meagre sales contributed greatly to BL's collapse in 1975.

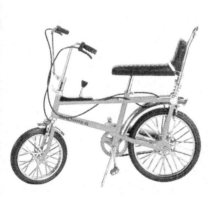

Raleigh Chopper
Shot to fame in the 70's when every child, and some adults, wanted one. It had a high back, long seat and motorbike rear wheel and was probably the first bike to have a centrally positioned gear shift.

Women Drivers

In 1974, Jill Viner became the first female bus driver for London Transport. She trained to become a bus driver at a centre in Chiswick in 1974, when London Transport were said to be 3,200 drivers short

While women had previously driven buses within bus depots during the Second World War, Viner was the first women to drive a bus in service in London. In the weeks after she started driving, it was reported that thirty women had applied to become bus drivers.

In 1978, Hannah Dadds completed a seven-week training course to qualify as a train driver and became the first female driver on the London Underground.

Hannah's sister Edna also joined the London Underground working first as a guard and then a driver. Hannah and Edna became the first all-female crew on the London Underground.

Concorde

The Anglo-French supersonic passenger airliner had a take-off speed of 220 knots (250mph) and a cruising speed of 1350mph – more than twice the speed of sound. With seating for 92 to 128 passengers, Concorde entered service in 1976 and operated for 27 years.

Twenty aircraft were built in total, including six prototypes and in the end, only Air France and British Airways purchased and flew them, due in great part to supersonic flights being restricted to ocean-crossing routes, to prevent sonic boom disturbance over land and populated areas. Concorde flew regular transatlantic flights from London and Paris to New York, Washington, Dulles in Virginia and Barbados and the BA Concorde made just under 50,000 flights and flew more than 2.5m passengers supersonically.

A typical London to New York crossing would take a little less than three and a half hours as opposed to about eight hours for a subsonic flight.

The aircraft was retired in 2003, three years after the crash of an Air France flight in which all passengers and crew were killed.

THE MAJOR NEWS STORIES

1980 - 1984

1980:

May: Mount St. Helens experiences a huge eruption that creates avalanches, explosions, large ash clouds, mudslides, and massive damage. 57 people are killed.

Dec: John Lennon, the former Beatle, age 40, is shot and killed by an obsessed fan in Manhattan.

1981:

July: Prince Charles marries Lady Diana Spencer at St Paul's Cathedral.

Margaret Thatcher's Government begins the privatisation of the Nationalised Industries.

1982:

Apr: Argentina invades the Falkland Islands and the UK retakes possession of them by the end of June.

May: Pope John Paul II visits the United Kingdom. It is the first visit by a reigning Pope

1983:

Apr: The £1 coin is introduced in the UK.

Jun: Margaret Thatcher wins a landslide victory for the Conservatives in the General Election, with a majority of 144.

Nov: The first United States cruise missiles arrive at RAF Greenham Common in Berkshire

1984:

Mar: The National Mineworkers Union led by Arthur Scargill, begin what will be a year-long strike against the National Coal Board's plans to shut 20 collieries

May: The Thames Barrier, designed to protect London from floods, is opened by9The Queen

1980: Mount St. Helens before and after the eruption. The top third of the mountain was blown away.

1982: EPCOT opened at Disney World in Florida, "...an experimental prototype community of tomorrow that will take its cue from the new ideas and technologies that are now emerging ... a showcase of the ingenuity and imagination of American free enterprise." - *Walt Disney*

1984: On 31 October, Indira Gandhi, Prime Minister of India, was killed by her Sikh bodyguards.
The assassination sparked four days of riots that left more than 8,000 Indian Sikhs dead in revenge attacks.

1985 - 1989

1985: On 1st January, Ernie Wise made the first, civilian, mobile phone call in the UK from outside the Dicken's Inn at St Katharine's Dock. Via the Vodafone network he called their office in Newbury on a VT1 which weighed 5.5kg.

1985:

Jan: The Internet's Domain Name System is created and the country code top-level domain .uk is registered in July.

Dec: The original charity "Comic Relief" is launched by Richard Curtis and Lenny Henry on Christmas Day,.

1986:

Apr: A Soviet Nuclear reactor at Chernobyl explodes causing the release of radioactive material across much of Europe.

Oct: The 'Big Bang' – the London Stock Exchange is deregulated allowing computerised share dealing.

1987:

Jan: Terry Waite, the special envoy of the Archbishop of Canterbury in Lebanon, is kidnapped in Beirut. He is held in captivity for 1,763 days until 1991.

Oct: Black Monday: Wall Street crash leads to £50,000,000,000 being wiped of the value of shares on the London stock exchange.

1988:

Dec: Suspected Libyan terrorist bomb explodes on Pan Am jet over Lockerbie in Scotland on December 21st killing all 259 on board and 11 on the ground.

Dec: Health Minister Edwina Currie states that most of Britain's egg production is infected with salmonella, causing an immediate nationwide slump in egg sales.

1989:

Apr: 94 fans are killed in the Hillsborough football stadium collapse in Sheffield. 3 more will die and over 300 are hospitalised.

Nov: The Fall of the Berlin Wall heralds the end of the Cold War and communism in East and Central Europe.

1987: Oct 15th: Weather-man Michael Fish: "Earlier on today, a woman rang the BBC and said she heard there was a hurricane on the way... well, if you're watching, don't worry, there isn't!". That night, hurricane force winds hit much of the South of England killing 23 people, bringing down an estimated 15 million trees and causing damage estimated at £7.3 billion.

THE HOME

A Busier Life

In the 1980's, life became more stressful, there were two recessions, divorce rates were increasing, women were exercising their rights and these years were the beginning of the end of the traditional family unit. With single parent families or both parents at work and a generally 'busier' life, there was a fundamental change to the family and home. There was also a lot more choice.

Many more 'lower cost' restaurants, chilled ready-made meals, instant foods such as Findus Crispy Pancakes, Pot Noodles or M&S Chicken Kievs and the, by now, ubiquitous tea bag, together with the consumer boom in electrical labour-saving devices from food processors and microwaves to dishwashers and automatic washing machines, sandwich toasters and jug kettles, all added up to more free time from housework and cooking.

Floral Décor

Flower patterns were all the rage in early 1980s home décor, with flower patterned upholstery and curtains to floral wallpapers taking over from the 70s woodchip paper.

Artex was still hugely popular on ceilings and walls, finished with the familiar stippled or swirled patterns and peach was *the* fashionable colour of choice for interior design schemes. Chintz curtains could have more layers, swags and tails than an onion! The bold reached the height of fashion with a red and black colour scheme, black ash furniture and a framed Ferrari print on the wall – with a bold wallpaper border at the ceiling which often clashed with the paper on the walls.

IN THE 1980s

The Telephone Answering Machine

There once was a time when, to use a telephone, both people had to be on the phone at the same time. You had to pick up the phone when it rang. The answering machine, one cassette tape for the outgoing message and one to record incoming calls, changed all that. By allowing people to take calls when they were away and respond to any message at a later time.

Children's Playtime

For children, toys of the early 80s had a bit of a 70s feel, Star Wars action figures, remote controlled cars and trucks, Barbie dolls and Action Men, but by 1983 there was a huge increase in toys like Transformers, Care Bears, a plethora of talking robot toys, My Little Pony, Teenage Mutant Ninja Turtles and Cabbage Patch Kids which was THE craze of 1983 – these odd looking 'little people' were the first images to feature on disposable 'designer' nappies!

Basic Atari video games evolved to Nintendo's NES game system and all of them competed with Apple and Sinclair home computers and personal Walkman stereos.

1980 - 1984

1980 "Who shot J.R.?" was an advertising catchphrase that CBS created to promote their TV show, 'Dallas', referring to the cliff hanger of the finale of the previous season. The episode, 'Who Done It?' aired in November with an estimated 83 million viewers tuning in.

MV Mi Amigo, the ship 'Radio Caroline', the pirate radio station, operates from, runs aground and sinks off Sheerness.

1981 A bronze statue of Charlie Chaplin, as his best loved character, The Tramp, is unveiled in Leicester Square.

1982 The D'Oyly Carte Opera Company gives its last performance at the end of a final London season, having been in near-continuous existence since 1875.

1983 Children's ITV is launched in Britain as a new branding for the late afternoon programming block on the ITV network.

1984 The comedian Tommy Cooper collapses and dies on stage from a heart attack during a live televised show, 'Live from Her Majesty's'.

Ted Hughes is appointed Poet Laureate and succeeds Sir John Betjeman. Philip Larkin had turned down the post.

1985 - 1989

1985 The Roux Brothers' Waterside Inn at Bray, Berkshire becomes the first establishment in the UK to be awarded three Michelin stars.

'Live Aid' pop concerts in London and Philadelphia raise over £50,000,000 for famine relief in Ethiopia.

1986 The Sun newspaper alleges that comedian Freddie Starr ate a live hamster.

More than 30m viewers watched the Christmas Day episode of 'East Enders' in which Den Watts serves the divorce papers on his wife Angie.

1987 Christie's auction house in London sells one of Vincent van Gogh's iconic Sunflowers paintings for £24,750,000 after a bidding war between two unidentified competitors bidding via telephone.

'The Simpsons' cartoon first appears as a series of animated short films on the 'Tracey Ullman Show' in the US.

1988 Salman Rushdie published 'The Satanic Verses' a work of fiction which caused a widespread furore and forced Rushdie to live in hiding out of fear for his life.

1989 Sky Television begins broadcasting as the first satellite TV service in Britain.

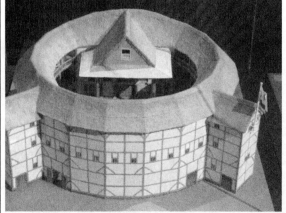

Remains of both The Rose, an Elizabethan playhouse, and the Globe Theatre are found in London.

IN THE 1980s

The Great Musical Revival

By the start of the 1980's, Britain was in recession and the West End Theatres were facing rising costs and falling audiences – until the revival of the Musical, led by Andrew Lloyd Webber.

In 1981, his first 'unlikely' musical **Cats** led by Elaine Paige, went on to be the first 'megamusical' spectacular in the West End and on Broadway.

It was followed in 1984 by **Starlight Express.**

By now, these shows were being enjoyed not only by home audiences but also, a massive 44% of tickets, were purchased by tourists.

In 1986, the **Phantom of the Opera** opened to overwhelmingly positive reviews.

In 1987 **Les Misérables** brought the Royal Shakespeare Company 's expertise in high drama to the musical which was set amidst the French Revolution and brought fame to its writers, Alain Boubill and Claude-Michel Schönberg fame and producer Cameron Mackintosh his millions.

Other hit musicals of the decade: Willy Russel's **Blood Brothers**, Noël Gay's revival of **Me and My Girl**, and Lloyd Webber's **Aspects of Love.**

FILMS

1980 - 1984

1980   The epic **The Empire Strikes Back** is released and is the highest-grossing film of the year, just as its predecessor, **Star Wars** was in 1977. However, the Oscar for Best Picture went to **Ordinary People**, the psychological drama depicting the disintegration of an upper middle-class family in Illinois.

1981 Chariots of Fire based on the true story of two British athletes, one Christian, one Jewish in the 1924 Olympics, won the Academy Awards.
The film's title was inspired by the line "Bring me my Chariot of fire!" from Blake's poem adapted as the hymn 'Jerusalem'.

1982   Spielberg's science fiction film of **ET the Extra Terrestrial** was a huge box office hit this year, the scene when the little green extra-terrestrial learns to speak, instilled "ET phone home" into the collective memory. The rather more down to earth biographical film of Mahatma Gandhi **Gandhi**, picked up the Best Film award.

 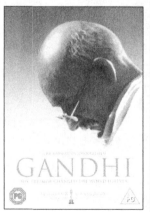

1983   There were many great British films this year including **Local Hero** and **Educating Rita, The Dresser** and Sean Connery playing Bond for the last time in **Never Say Never Again.** It was the American, **Terms of Endearment** that won the Oscars.

1984   Amadeus the fictionalised story of the composer Wolfgang Amadeus Mozart and a supposed rivalry with Italian composer Antonio Salieri, featuring much of Mozart's music, won the imagination of the audiences and the Best Film of the Year award too.

1985 - 1989

1985   Spielberg's 'coming of age' epic starring Whoopi Goldberg in her breakthrough role, **The Color Purple**, was nominated for eleven Academy Awards but failed to achieve a single win. The prize went to Meryl Streep and Robert Redford in the romantic drama, **Out of Africa.**

1986   The first of Oliver Stone's trilogy based on his experiences in the Vietnam war, **Platoon** picks up this year's Oscar for Best Film, beating two British nominations, **A Room with a View** and **The Mission.** This was also the year of the Australian box office runaway success, **Crocodile Dundee.**

1987   The thriller **Fatal Attraction** attracted both favourable reviews and controversy. It put the phrase 'bunny boiler' into the urban dictionary.

1988   Glenn Close was nominated for Best Actress for her role as the Marquise de Merteuil who plots revenge against her ex-lover, in **Dangerous Liaisons**. Dustin Hoffman and Tom Cruise starred in **Rainman**, the winner of Best Film of the year.

1989   Unusually, it was a PG rated film, **Driving Miss Daisy** that won the Academy Award this year, a gentle, heartwarming comedy which had the serious themes of racism and anti-semitism at its heart. Jessica Tandy at age 81, won Best Actress, the oldest winner to do so.

David Puttnam, Baron Puttnam of Queensgate (1997)

The 1980s saw the release of several films by the British producer, David Puttnam, beginning with, in 1981, his most successful film up until that time, **Chariots of Fire**.

His next big success was **Local Hero** the comedy drama, set on the west coast of Scotland where an American oil company wishes to purchase a local village and surrounding area.

Next, in 1984, came the acclaimed **Cal**, a young man on the fringes of the IRA who falls in love with a Catholic woman whose husband, a Protestant policeman, had been killed by the IRA one year earlier. Entered into the Cannes Film Festival, Helen Mirren won Best Actress.

Also in 1984, Puttnam produced **The Killing Fields**, a harrowing biographical drama about the Khmer Rouge in Cambodia, based on the experiences of a Cambodian journalist and an American journalist. This film received seven Oscar nominations and won three, most notably Best Supporting Actor for Haing S. Ngor who had no previous acting experience.

Puttnam's career spanned the 1960s to the 1990s and his films have won 10 Oscars, 31 BAFTAs, 13 Golden Globes, nine Emmys, four David di Donatellos in Italy and the Palme d'Or at Cannes.

FASHION

A Fashion Statement

The mid to late 80s was the time to 'make a statement'. The mass media took over fashion trends completely and fashion magazines, TV shows and music videos all played a part in dictating the latest bold fashions.

There was a huge emphasis on bright colours, huge shoulder pads, power suits which gave an exaggerated silhouette like an upside-down triangle, flashy skirts and spandex leggings, velour, leg warmers and voluminous parachute pants.

We wore iconic oversized plastic hoop earrings, rubber bracelets and shiny chain necklaces and huge sunglasses giving faces the appearance of large flies. Men and women alike made their hair 'big' with or without the ubiquitous teased perm and for the girls, glossy pink lips, overly filled-in brows, rainbow-coloured eyeshadows and exaggerated blusher were on trend.

Men too joined in with style and sported oversized blazers with shiny buttons, pinstripe two-piece suits and sweaters, preferably from Ralph Lauren, draped over the shoulders.

Polka Dots

Although not new to the 80s - Disney's Minnie Mouse was first seen in the 1920's wearing the red and white dottie print - polka dots were also very popular.

Bands such as The Beat used them in their music videos and well-known celebrities including Madonna and Princess Diana loved the cool look of polka dot dresses and tops.

When teamed with the oversized earrings of the decade and big hair, whilst bucking the trend for bright, gaudy colours, they still "made a statement".

Carolina Herrera used polka dots on most of her dresses during the late 1980s and early 1990s and it remains a key print in her collections, a classic.

As Marc Jacobs, the American designer famously said, "There is never a wrong time for a polka dot."

Labels, logos and idols

Pale blue, distressed jeans were the fashionable 'street wear', worn semi fitted and held with a statement belt at the natural waistline. When the boy band Bros came along in 1988, wearing jeans ripped at the knee coupled with leather, slip on loafers, teens up and down the country enthusiastically took the scissors to their own jeans, and ripped, frayed or shredded them.
.

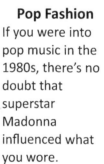

Pop Fashion

If you were into pop music in the 1980s, there's no doubt that superstar Madonna influenced what you wore.

Feet also presented a branding opportunity, Patrick Cox had celebrities make his loafers universally desired, and, often credited with kicking off the whole fashion sneaker movement, Nike Air 'Jordans' – named after basketball star, Michael Jordan – were launched in 1985. If you couldn't have them, then high-top Reebok sneakers were also the pinnacle of style -- as were Adidas Superstar kicks and matching tracksuits.

LEISURE

The Fitness Craze

The 1980's had a fitness craze. Celebrities made aerobics videos and endorsed weight loss products and equipment. Health Clubs and Gyms became the place to be and to be seen but were predominantly for men so for women who wanted to exercise in the privacy of their own home, by the mid '80s, there were very few households that didn't own at least one well-worn VHS copy of **'Jane Fonda's Workout'**.

Her 1982 video sold more than 17 million copies, with the actress wearing a striped and belted leotard, violet leggings and leg warmers, big, big hair and in full make-up and working up a sweat to some heavy synth music, inspired a whole generation.

At home, between 1983 and 1987, Britain's answer to Jane Fonda, Diana Moran **'The Green Goddess',** appeared on TV screens wearing her trade-mark green leotard telling millions of BBC Breakfast viewers to 'wake up and shape up' with her aerobics routines.

What's On Telly?

Television was a very large part of leisure in the 1980s and with the massive growth in video recorders, the whole family had more control over what they watched and when they watched it.

It was the decade when the huge American 'soaps' **Dallas** and **Dynasty** dominated the ratings and influenced popular debate as well as fashions. In Britain there was a rash of police dramas and the introduction of female detectives in both BBC **'Juliet Bravo'** and ITV **'The Gentle Touch'**. They also covered the land, **'Taggart'** in Scotland, **'Bergerac'** in Jersey, **'The Chinese Detective'** in London and **'Inspector Morse'** in Oxford.

Channel 4 launched in 1982 with its first programme being **'Countdown',** Breakfast TV began in 1983, in 1980s television produced 'historic' shared experiences, **'Who Shot JR'** in Dallas watched by 80 million, the finale of **MASH**, 'Goodbye, Farewell and Amen', by more than 100 million, 30 million tuned in to watch 'Dirty Den' serve his wife 'Angie' with the divorce papers in East Enders and 27 million watched the episode after Alan Bradley tried to kill Rita Fairclough in **Coronation Street.**

IN THE 1980s

What Was New?

Whilst the 80s made huge advances in technology for leisure, Game Boy and Nintendo, VCRs and CDs, disposable cameras and brick shaped mobile phones too, there were other innovations.

In the 'yuppie' years of 'spend, spend, spend', the first smart chip-enabled credit cards were busy being swiped for BMX bikes, Trivial Pursuit and Rubik's Cubes.

Nike told us to 'Just Do It' and we wondered how we'd ever managed without Post-It Notes and disposable contact lenses.

What the world did not want however, was New Coke. Coca Cola changed their classic formula for a sweeter one which received an extremely poor response.

It was one of the worst marketing blunders ever because for the public, this tampered recipe 'Just wasn't it!'. The company brought back the original Coke and sold this new formula as the 'New Coke' till the early 90s.

MUSIC

1980 - 1984

1980   Johnny Logan won the Eurovision Song Contest for Ireland with **What's Another Year** and was No 1 in the UK charts for two weeks in May. He won again in 1987 with **Hold Me Now**.

Abba had their first No 1 of the year with **Winner Takes it All** followed in November with **Super Trouper.**

1981   Two singles stayed at the top of the charts for 5 weeks each this year. First Adam and the Ants with **Stand and Deliver** and in December, The Human League with **Don't You Want Me** which was also the best-selling single of the year.

1982   The year's best seller was Dexey's Midnight Runners and **Come on Eileen**, their second No 1 in the UK. The words express the feelings of an adolescent dreaming of being free from the strictures of a Catholic society and sounded unlike the other hits of the era, no synthesiser, but a banjo, accordion, fiddle and saxophone.

1983   **Karma Chameleon** by the 'New Romantic' band, Culture Club, fronted by singer Boy George, whose androgynous style of dressing caught the attention of the public and the media, became the second Culture Club single to reach No 1 and stayed there for six weeks, also becoming the best-selling single of the year.

1984 **Two Tribes**, the anti-war song by the Liverpool band, Frankie Goes to Hollywood, was a phenomenal success helped by a wide range of remixes and supported by an advertising campaign depicting the band as members of the Red Army. It entered the charts at No 1 and stayed there for nine consecutive weeks, making it the the longest-running No 1 single of the decade.

1985 - 1989

1985   The best seller this year was **The Power of Love** sung by Jennifer Rush. No 1 for five weeks, Rush became the first female artist ever to have a million-selling single in the UK.

Wham and George Michael, having had three No 1's last year, **Wake Me Up Before You Go-Go, Careless Whisper** and **Freedom**, managed only one this year, **I'm Your Man.**

1986   Holiday disco songs such as **Agadoo**, topped the charts for three weeks.

The Christmas No 1 spot was held for four weeks by a reissue, three years after his death, of Jackie Wilson's **Reet Petite (The Sweetest Girl in Town)**.

1987   Two singles stayed at No 1 for five weeks, the best-selling of the year, **Never Gonna Give You Up** by Rick Astley and **China in Your Hand** by T'Pau, Carol Decker's group named after the character in Star Trek.

1988   Already known from the Australian soap opera, 'Neighbours', Kylie Minogue burst into the UK charts with **I Should Be So Lucky** from her debut studio album. The song became a worldwide hit.

Cliff Richard was back at No 1 after quite a break, with **Mistletoe and Wine** for the Christmas market.

1989   It was a good year for the Australian golden couple, Jason Donovan and Kylie Minogue. One No 1 together, **Especially For You,** two for Jason, **Too Many Broken Hearts** and **Sealed With a Kiss**, and one for Kylie, **Hand on Your Heart.**

Ride on Time from the debut album by Italian house music group, Black Box, topped the charts for six weeks and sold the most copies of the year.

IN THE 1980s

Charity Fund Raisers

The 80's saw many 'not for profit' Charity Singles, the best-known being Bob Geldorf and Midge Ure's 'Band Aid' and then 'Live Aid', formed to raise money for famine relief in Ethiopia, who released **Do They Know Its Christmas**, for the first time, in December 1984. It stayed at the top of the charts for five weeks and was the best-selling record of the decade having been released again in 1989.

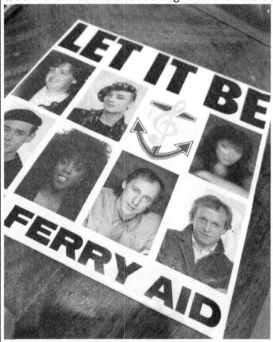

A less well-known charity, 'Ferry Aid', recorded the Beatles' song, **Let It Be** in 1987. This followed the sinking of the ferry 'Ms Herald of the Free' at Zeebrugge, killing 193 passengers and crew. The recording was organised by The Sun newspaper, after it had sold cheap tickets for the ferry on that day.

Tears For Fears, Duran Duran and Simple Minds got together and released **Everybody Wants to Rule the World** in 1986 in support of 'Sport Aid', a campaign to help tackle famine in Africa.

In 1983, Michael Jackson redefined the style, course, and possibilities of music videos. He released **Thriller** and made recording history. The album spent thirty-seven weeks at No 1 on the US Billboard chart. By early 1984, thirty million copies had been sold, and it was still selling at a rate of more than a million copies a week worldwide.

SCIENCE AND NATURE

The Compact Disc

In 1981, Kieran Prendiville on BBC's 'Tomorrow's World', demonstrated the CD and wondered, "Whether or not there is a market for these discs, remains to be seen." Well, on the 25th anniversary of its first public release in 1982, it was estimated that 200 billion CDs had been sold worldwide so I guess the answer was "Yes"!

At the end of the 70's, Philips and Sony had teamed up to begin working on CDs for the public and decided on a thin, shiny and circular storage disc, which could hold about 80 minutes of music. The disc had a diameter of 120mm, Sony having insisted that the longest musical performance, Beethoven's entire 9th Symphony at 74 minutes, should fit. A CD could hold an immense amount of data, much more than the vinyl record or the cassette and was perfectly portable.

The first commercial CD to be pressed was **Visitors** by Abba, followed quickly by the first album, Billy Joel's **52nd Street**. The biggest selling CD of all time is the Eagles 1976 **Their Greatest Hits** album, which has sold over 38 million copies.

UFOs in the Forest

On 26 December 1980, several US Airforce personnel stationed near the east gate at RAF Woodbridge, reported they had seen "lights" apparently descending into nearby Rendlesham Forest. They initially thought it was a downed aircraft but, upon investigation, they saw what they described as a glowing object, metallic in appearance, with coloured lights.

After daybreak on the morning of December 27, servicemen returned to a small clearing in the forest and found three small impressions on the ground in a triangular pattern, as well as burn marks and broken branches on nearby trees.

The 'Rendlesham Forest Incident' made headline news and theories suggest it was either an actual alien visitation, a secret military aircraft, a misinterpretation of natural lights, the beam of Orfordness Lighthouse, or just a hoax.

In The 1980s

Mount St Helens

In March 1980 a series of volcanic explosions began at Mount St Helens, Washington in the US, culminating in a major explosive eruption on May 18. The eruption column rose 80,000 feet (15 miles) into the atmosphere and deposited ash over 11 states and into some Canadian provinces. At the same time, snow, ice, and entire glaciers on the volcano melted, forming a series of large volcanic mudslides that reached as far as 50 miles to the southwest. Thermal energy released during the eruption was equal to 26 megatons of TNT.

Regarded as the most significant and disastrous volcanic eruption in the country's history, about 57 people were killed, hundreds of square miles were reduced to wasteland, thousands of animals were killed, and Mount St. Helens was left with a crater on its north side. The area is now preserved as the Mount St Helens National Volcanic Monument.

One day before the eruption and several months afterwards. About a third of the mountain was blown away.

SPORT

1980 Eight days after the **Boston marathon**, Rosie Ruiz, a Cuban American, is disqualified as the winner 'in the fastest time ever run by a woman'. Investigations found that she did not run the entire course, joining about a half-mile before the finish.

Larry Holmes defeats Muhammed Ali to retain boxing's **WBC World Heavyweight** title. It is Ali's last world title bout.

1981 At **Wimbledon**, John McEnroe defeats Björn Borg to gain his 3rd career Grand Slam title and his 1st Wimbledon title.

In the ladies' final, Chris Evert Lloyd defeats Hana Mandlíková to gain her 12th career Grand Slam title and her third and last Wimbledon title.

1982 In June, at Pebble Beach, the American Tom Watson wins **The US Open** and a month later, at Royal Troon, he wins the **The Open.** He is only the third golfer, at that time, to win both Championships in the same year.

In Spain, Italy defeat West Germany in the **World Cup Final.** The tournament features the first penalty shoot-out in the World Cup competition.

1983 The **FA Cup** is won by Manchester United who, having drawn the first final with Brighton and Hove Albion, win the replay, 4-0.

1984 John McEnroe has his best season. He wins 13 singles tournaments, including **Wimbledon** where he loses just one set on his way to his third Wimbledon singles title. This includes a straight set win over Jimmy Connors in the final. He also wins the **US Open**, capturing the year-end number one ranking.

1985 Ireland is the championship winner in the **Rugby Five Nations** winning their tenth solo title, but it would prove to be their last for 24 years, until their Grand Slam in 2009.

Alain Prost becomes the **F1 World Champion** Driver, winning five of the sixteen Grand Prix. The first ever world championship **Australian Grand Prix** is held on a street circuit in Adelaide.

1986 In the **World Cup**, Argentina wins by defeating West Germany 3-2. Diego Maradona is the biggest star of the event, and his 'Hand of God' goal is well remembered. The event also sees the introduction of the 'Mexican Wave'.

1987 In **Cricket** the Indian opening batsman, Sunil Gavaskar reaches 10,000 test runs to become the first ever player to score this many. In the **Cricket World Cup** played for the first time outside Britain, in India, Australia win by defeating their arch-rivals, England.

1988 The **FA Cup** is won by Wimbledon FC's 'Crazy Gang', who defeat league champions Liverpool through a headed goal by Lawrie Sanchez. This is Wimbledon's only FA Cup title during its lifetime.

1989 On heavy, almost un-raceable ground, the iconic grey Desert Orchid, ridden by Simon Sherwood, in a race that defined his illustrious career, wins the **Cheltenham Gold Cup**. In 2005 this was voted the 'Greatest Race of All Time' by Racing Post readers.

You cannot be serious!

During the 1981 Wimbledon Championships, John McEnroe uttered what has become the most immortal phrase in tennis, if not all sport, when he screamed "you cannot be serious" at a Wimbledon umpire while disputing a line call. Already called "Superbrat" by the British tabloid press for his verbal volleys during previous Wimbledon matches, it was in a first-round match against fellow American Tom Gullikson, who was serving at 15-30 and 1-1 in the first set when a McEnroe shot was called out. Approaching the umpire, he said: "Chalk came up all over the place, you can't be serious man." Then, his anger rising, he bawled the words that would stay with him for a lifetime and find its way into the sporting annals. "You cannot be serious," he screamed. "That ball was on the line".

On the receiving end of the tirade was umpire Edward James, who eventually responded by politely announcing: "I'm going to award a point against you Mr McEnroe." It made little difference, McEnroe went on to win in straight sets and two weeks later had his final victory over Bjorn Borg.

Torvill and Dean

On Valentine's Day 1984, Jayne Torvill and Christopher Dean made history at the Winter Olympics in Sarajevo and set a new standard for world class figure skating. The duo from Nottingham, were the last to perform in their category and their performance, self-choreographed to 4½ minutes of Ravel's Bolero, was seamless, elegant and hypnotic. As they sank to the ice in the dramatic finale, the whole stadium stood and applauded. Their dance had captured the world's imagination and won Gold. The unanimous scores of 6.0 for artistic impression made them the highest-scoring figure skaters of all time.

Their routine, made Ravel's Boléro with its steady crescendo and repeated snare-drum rhythms, synonymous with figure-skating.

British Car Manufacturing

Gallery:

The 1980s was still a busy period for British car manufacturers and many of the bestselling cars of the decade were made in Britain.

The top 10 cars were:
1. Ford Escort
2. Vauxhall Cavalier
3. Ford Fiesta
4. Austin Metro
5. Ford Sierra (which replaced the
6. Ford Cortina)
6. Vauxhall Astra
7. Ford Orion
8. Austin Maestro
9. Vauxhall Nova
10. Ford Grenada

However the list of the **'Most influential Cars of the 1980s'** shows how the British car industry was soon to be decimated. The list includes:
Audi Quatrro; Porsche 944: Renault Scenic; Mercedes 190; BMW 3 Series; VW Golf; Volvo 240 Estate; Peugeot 205 and the Toyota Carolla.

The Ford Cortina was replaced by the Ford Sierra in 1982

The Ford Fiesta has been ever popular right up to the present day.

The Austin Metro was the replacement for the mini.

The VW Golf had front wheel drive and built a reputation for quality and reliability

The Porsche 944 was the choice of the newly rich 'yuppies' of the 1980s

Clunk Click Every Trip

Although car manufacturers had been obliged to install seatbelts since 1965, it was not until January 1983 that the law requiring all drivers to wear their belts came into force. In spite of a great deal of 'grumbling' and more, ranging from *"the erosion of our civil liberties, another example of the Nanny State",* to *"its uncomfortable, restrictive and creases my clothes"* and horror stories of crash victims being *"hanged"* by their belts or suffering greater injury, 90% of drivers and front seat passengers were observed to be wearing seat belts soon after the law came into effect – and these rates have been sustained since then. There was an immediate 25% reduction in driver fatalities and a 29 per cent reduction in fatal injuries among front seat passengers.

In 1989 it became compulsory for all children under 14 to wear a seat belt in the rear and when seatbelt wearing became compulsory for all rear-seat occupants in 1991, there was an immediate increase from 10% to 40% in observed seat belt wearing rates.

IN THE 1980s

Aviation

When Airbus designed the A300 during the late 1960s and early 1970s, it envisaged a broad family of airliners with which to compete against Boeing and Douglas, the two established US aerospace manufacturers.

The launch of the A320 in 1987 guaranteed the status of Airbus as a major player in the aircraft market – the aircraft had over 400 orders before it first flew.

Motorcycles

Only 3000 Honda FVR750R motorcycles were made, race bred machines with lights thrown on to make them road legal and sold to the public. The first batch of 1000 sold out instantly. With a top speed of 153mph the V-four powered RC30 was one of the fastest sports bike of the decade but it was the track proven frame that meant it handled like a genuine racer. It also had a soundtrack to die for and was absolutely beautiful.

The Docklands Light Railway

The Docklands Light Railway was first opened in August 1987 as an automated, light metro system to serve the redeveloped Docklands area of London as a cheap public transport solution. The original network comprised two routes - Tower Gateway to Island Gardens and Stratford to Island Gardens and was mainly elevated on disused railway viaducts, new concrete viaducts and disused surface railway tracks. The trains were fully automated, controlled by computer, and had no driver.

They did however have a "Train Captain" who was responsible for patrolling the train, checking tickets, making announcements and controlling the doors. They could take control of the train should there be an equipment failure or emergency. The first generation of rolling stock comprised eleven lightweight units and the stations, mostly of a common design, constructed from standard components and usually featuring a short half-cylindrical, glazed, blue canopy, were designed specifically for these single articulated trains. The 15 stations were all above ground and needed no staff.

1990 - 1994

1990:
Feb: Nelson Mandela is released from prison in South Africa, after 27 years behind bars.

Nov: Margaret Thatcher resigns as Prime Minister. At 11 years, she was the longest serving PM of the 20th Century.

1991:
Jan: The Gulf War begins, as the Royal Air Force joins Allied aircraft in bombing raids on Iraq

Apr: After a year of protests and riots, the government confirms that the Poll Tax is to be replaced by a new Council Tax in 1993.

1992:
Apr: At the General Election the Conservative Party are re-elected for a fourth term under John Major.

Nov: Part of Windsor Castle is gutted in a fire causing millions of pounds worth of damage and The Queen describes this year as an Annus Horribilis.

1993:
Apr: The Queen announces that Buckingham Palace will open to the public for the first time

Sep: The UK Independence Party which supports the breakaway from the EU is formed.

Dec: Diana, Princess of Wales. withdraws from public life.

1994:
Mar: The Church of England ordains its first female priests.

May: The Channel Tunnel between Britain and France is officially opened.

Nov: The first UK National Lottery draw takes place.

1992: The 'Maastricht Treaty' was concluded between the 'then' twelve member states of the European Communities. This foundation treaty of the EU announced a new stage in the process of European integration, shared citizenship and a single currency. There were two headquarters, one in Brussels and one in Strasbourg,

info buzz
Tim Berners-Lee

1991: The internet already existed but no one had thought of a way of how to link one document directly to another until in 1989, British scientist Tim Berners-Lee, invented the WorldWideWeb. The www. was introduced in 1991 as the first web browser and the first website went online in August.

1995 - 1999

1995:
Feb: Barings Bank, the UK's oldest merchant bank, collapses after rogue trader Nick Leeson loses $1.4 billion.

Apr: All telephone area dialling codes are changed in the UK.

Aug: Pubs in England are permitted to remain open throughout Sunday afternoon.

1996:
Feb: The Prince and Princess of Wales agree to divorce more than three years after separating.

Jul: Dolly the Sheep becomes the first mammal to be successfully cloned from an adult cell.

1997:
May: Tony Blair wins a landslide General Election for the Labour Party.

Aug: Princess Diana is killed in a car crash in Paris. Dodi Fayed, the heir to the Harrods empire is killed with her

1998:
Mar: Construction on the Millenium Dome begins. It will be the centre piece for a national celebration.

Apr: The Good Friday Agreement between the UK and Irish governments is signed.

1999:
Apr: A minimum wage is introduced in the UK – set at £3.60 an hour for workers over 21, and £3 for workers under 21

Jun: Construction of the Millenium Dome is finished and in October, the London Eye begins to be lifted into position.

1997: The UK transfers sovereignty of Hong Kong, the largest remaining British colony, to the People's Republic of China as the 99 years lease on the territory formally ends.

1999: On 1st January, the new European currency, the Euro is launched and some 320 million people from eleven European countries begin carrying the same money in their wallets.
Britain's Labour government preferred to stay with the pound sterling instead.

THE HOME

Home life in the 1990s was changing again. Family time was not cherished as it had once been, children had a lot more choice and were becoming more independent with their own TVs programmes, personal computers, music systems, mobile phones and, crucially, the introduction of the world wide web, which meant life would never be the same again.

After school and weekend organised activities for the young burgeoned, with teenagers able to take advantage of the fast-food chains, or eating at different times, meaning no more family eating together. Families 'lived in separate' rooms, there were often two televisions so different channels could be watched and children wanted to play with their Nintendos or listen to their Walkmans in their own rooms. Their rooms were increasingly themed, from Toy Story to Athena posters, a ceiling full of sticker stars that illuminated a room with their green glow and somewhere in the house, room had to be made for the computer desk.

Track lighting was an easy way to illuminate a room without relying on multiple lamps and it became a popular feature in many '90s homes along with corner baths – most of which also had a water jet function which suddenly turned your bath into a low-budget jacuzzi!

In 1990, 68% of UK households owned at least one car, and the use of 'out of town' supermarkets and shopping centres, where just about anything and everything could be purchased in the same area, meant that large weekly or even monthly shops could be done in a single outing and combined with the huge increase in domestic freezers and ready prepared foods, time spent in the kitchen and cooking could be greatly reduced.

Over 80% of households owned a washing machine and 50%, a tumble dryer, so the need to visit the laundrette all but disappeared and instead of "Monday is washing day", the family's laundry could be carried out on an 'as and when' basis. All contributing to an increase in leisure time.

Nearly three-quarters of homes had microwave cookers and for working women who did not want to do their own cleaning, Merry Maids set up their home cleaning franchise in the UK in 1990 and many other companies followed suit.

Commuting

In Great Britain at the beginning of the 1990s, the *average* one-way commute to work was 38 minutes in London, 33 minutes in the south-east, and 21 minutes in the rest of the country. By the end of the decade, full-time workers commuting to and from London, had lost an additional 70 minutes per week of home time to commuting but, by contrast, outside the south-east of Britain, there was no increase in commuting time over the decade. In the south-east, 30% of workers took at least 45 minutes to get to work. In the rest of the country, only 10% did.

ART AND CULTURE

1990 - 1994

1990 In Rome, on the eve of the final of the FIFA World Cup, the Three Tenors sing together for the first time. The event is broadcast live and watched worldwide by millions of people. The highlight is Luciano Pavarotti's performance of Nessun Dorma.
The first Hampton Court Palace Flower Show takes place.

1991 Dame Margot Fonteyn, the Royal Ballet's Prima Ballerina, dies in Panama City, exactly 29 years after her premiere with Rudolf Nureyev who made his debut in 'Giselle'.

1992 Damien Hirst's "Shark", featuring a preserved shark, is first shown at an exhibition at the Saatchi Gallery in London.
Under the new Further and Higher Education Act, Polytechnics are allowed to become new Universities and award degrees of their own.
The last edition of Punch, the UK's oldest satirical magazine since 1841, is published.

1993 Bookmakers cut their odds on the monarchy being abolished by the year 2000 from 100 to 1 to 50 to 1.
QVC launches the first television shopping channel in the UK.

1994 The Duchess of Kent joins the Roman Catholic Church, the first member of the Royal Family to convert to Catholicism for more than 300 years.
The Sunday Trading Act comes into full effect, permitting retailers to trade on Sundays but restricts larger stores to a maximum of six hours, between 10 am and 6 pm.

1995 - 1999

1995 The first ever World Book Day was held on 23rd April, picked to celebrate the anniversary of William Shakespeare's death.

The BBC begins regular Digital Audio Broadcasting from Crystal Palace.

1996 Shortly after publication of the Italian edition of his book 'The Art Forger's Handbook', English-born art forger, Eric Hebborn is beaten to death in Rome.
The Stone of Scone is installed in Edinburgh Castle 700 years after it was removed from Scotland by King Edward I of England.

1997 The Teletubbies caused a sensation when they appeared on BBC TV. They were the most sought-after toy of the year.
The reconstruction of the Elizabethan Globe Theatre, called Shakespeare's Globe opens in London with a production of Shakespeare's 'Henry V'.

1998 Britain's largest sculpture, the Angel of the North by Anthony Gormley is installed at Low Eighton, Gateshead.
More than 15,000 people attend a tribute concert held for Diana, Princess of Wales, at her family home, Althorp Park.

1999 The children's picture book, 'The Gruffalo' by Julia Donaldson is first published.

Media coverage for the Turner Prize was dominated by extreme critical response to Tracey Emin's work 'My Bed' – an installation of her unmade bed, complete with dirty sheets and detritus.

IN THE 1990s

1997: 'Harry Potter and the Philosopher's Stone' by JK Rowling made its debut in June. The initial edition of this first book in the series, comprised 500 copies and the novel has gone on to sell in excess of 120 million. The success of the whole Harry Potter phenomenon is well known, and there have been less expected benefits too. Certainly, before the films, children loved reading the books and boosted the reported numbers of children reading and indeed, reading longer books.

The perception of boarding schools, often associated with misery and cruel, spartan regimes was changed for some by Hogwarts School of Witchcraft and Wizardry. The sense of excitement, community and friendship of the children, the camaraderie of eating together and playing together, made going away to school more appealing for many.

The amazing visual effects used in the films were instrumental in persuading Hollywood to consider UK technical studios and raised the number of visual effects Oscar nominations for British companies significantly.

1997: The Guggenheim Museum of modern and contemporary art, designed by Canadian-American architect Frank Gehry, opened in Bilbao. The building represents an architectural landmark of innovating design, a spectacular structure.

The museum was originally a controversial project. Bilbao's industry, steel and shipbuilding was dying, and the city decided to regenerate to become a modern technological hub of the Basque region, and the controversy was, instead of an office block or factory, the centre piece would be a brand-new art gallery.

It is a spectacular building, more like a sculpture with twisted metal, glass, titanium and limestone, a futuristic setting for fine works of art. The gamble paid off, in the first twenty years, the museum attracted more than 19 million visitors with 70% from outside Spain. Foreign tourists continue to travel through the Basque country bringing a great economic boost to the region and Bilbao itself, has transformed from a grimy post-industrial town to a tourist hotspot.

FILMS

1990 - 1994

1990 It was Oscar time for an epic western this year and **Dances With Wolves**, directed and starring Kevin Costner with seven Academy Awards, won Best Picture and Best Director. It is one of only three Westerns to win the Oscar for Best Picture, the other two being **Cimmaron** in 1931 and **Unforgotten** in **1992**.

1991 *"Well, Clarice - have the lambs stopped screaming?"* wrote Dr Hannibal Lecter to the young FBI trainee, Clarice Starling. The thriller, **The Silence of the Lambs**, about a cannibalistic serial killer, scared audiences half to death and won the Best Picture Award.

1992 The nominations for the Academy Awards held some serious themes. **The Crying Game** was set against the backdrop of the 'troubles' in Northern Ireland. There was a blind retired Army officer in **Scent of a Woman**, rising troubles in colonial French Vietnam in **Indochine** and the invasion of Panama in **The Panama Deception**.

1993 The acclaimed **Schindler's List** won Best Picture with stiff competition from **The Piano** which won Best Original Screenplay and Robin Williams as **Mrs Doubtfire** which became the second highest grossing film of the year.

1994 Disney's animated musical **The Lion King** made the most money this year, but **Forest Gump** took the prize for Best Picture. The British film **Four Weddings and a Funeral** was a huge success and brought WH Auden's beautiful poem 'Funeral Blues' into the limelight.

1995 - 1999

1995 The tense, amazingly technically correct, story of the ill-fated **Apollo 13** quest to land on the moon failed to win the top Oscar, beaten by Mel Gibson in **Braveheart**, the American take on the story of William Wallace and the first Scottish war of independence against England.

1996 The English Patient a romantic war drama won the Best Picture, up against Mike Leigh's **Secrets and Lies** which won the Best British Film.

1997 The blockbuster **Titanic** was the film of the year. The combination of romance and disaster proving irresistible. Harland & Wolfe, the builders of RMS Titanic shared blueprints they thought were lost with the crew to produce the scale models, computer-generated imagery and a reconstruction of the ship itself, to re-create the sinking.

1998 Shakespeare in Love, a fictional love affair between Shakespeare and Viola de Lesseps whilst he is writing Romeo and Juliet was hugely popular and won seven Oscars.

1999 In **American Beauty,** Kevin Spacey plays Lester Burnham, an unhappy executive whose midlife awakening is the crux of the story. Bad as he thinks his life is, he cannot not stop seeing the beauty of the world around him.

**"Fear can hold you prisoner,
Hope can set you free."**

TIM ROBBINS   MORGAN FREEMAN

In 1994, Tim Robbins and Morgan Freeman starred **The Shawshank Redemption**, an inspirational, life-affirming and uplifting, old-fashioned style prison film and character study in the ilk of 'The Birdman of Alcatraz'. Set in a fictional, oppressive Shawshank State Prison in Maine, two imprisoned men bond over the years, in a tale of friendship, patience, hope, survival and ultimately finding solace and eventual redemption through acts of common decency.

The film was initially a box office disappointment. Many reasons were put forward for its failure at the time, including a general unpopularity of prison films, its lack of female characters and even the title, which was considered to be confusing. However, it was nominated for seven Academy Awards, failed to win a single Oscar, but this raised awareness and increased the film's popularity such that it is now preserved in the US National Film Registry as "culturally, historically, or aesthetically significant".

Six men. With nothing to lose. Who dared to go...

THE YEAR'S MOST REVEALING COMEDY.

The Full Monty

In 1997 whilst huge audiences were crying over Kate Winslet and Leonardo di Caprio in **Titanic,** equally huge audiences were laughing at the story of six unemployed men in Sheffield, four of them former steel workers, who are in dire need of cash and who decide to emulate 'The Chippendales' dance, striptease troupe. They devise a dance act with their difference being, that Gaz decides their show must be even better than the originals and declares to the friends that they will go 'the full Monty' – they will strip all the way. Although primarily a comedy, the film touches on several serious subjects too, including unemployment, father's rights – Gaz is unable to pay maintenance to his estranged wife and she is seeking sole custody of his son – and working-class culture, depression and suicide. The film was a huge success as it ultimately is about humanity and the problems people all over the world struggle with.

FASHION

SUPERMODELS

The original supermodels of the 1980s, Linda Evangelista, Naomi Campbell, Christy Turlington and Cindy Crawford were joined later by Claudia Schiffer and then Kate Moss to become the "Big Six". Models used to be categorised as 'print' or 'runway' but the "Big Six" showed that they could do it all, catwalk, print campaigns, magazine covers and even music videos and they became pop 'icons' in their own right. The models were also known for their earning capacity, one famous remark from Linda Evangelista, "We don't wake up for less than $10,000 a day!"

But with the popularity of grunge, came a shift away from the fashion for feminine curves and wholesome looking women, and in came the rise of a new breed of fragile, individual-looking and often younger, models, epitomised by Kate Moss. Her waif-like thinness and delicacy complemented the unkempt look that was popular in the early nineties and a new phrase 'heroin chic' described the down-at-heel settings for fashion shoots presented in magazines. By the end of the decade however, attitudes had shifted and concern about the health of the skeletal model was becoming a source of great debate.

GOTH

During the mid to late 1990s, the sub-culture of gothic fashion peaked in popularity. Their distinguishing features were black, antiquated and homogeneous features. Long black hair, black eyeliner, black nail polish, silver jewellery and face piercings teamed with long, black leather coats worn over frilly shirts and tight black trousers or even fetish wear. Girls often wore corsets, lace gloves and short leather skirts, velvets and fishnets with accessories often borrowed from the punk fashion such as spiked wristbands and chokers.

Siouxsie Sioux was particularly influential, since her gig at Futurama in 1980 she had been influencing how the music with the Banshees, would dress and she may well have been inspired by Theda Bara, the 1910s silent film, femme fatale, renowned for her dark eyeshadow and 'Vamp' look.

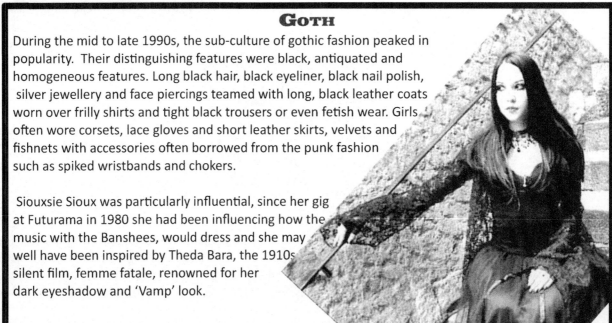

IN THE 1990s

GRUNGE

Grunge was a style for the young that emerged in Seattle in the late 1980s and by the early 90s had spread across the world. Made popular by bands such as Nirvana, it was a fashion for both men and women. The look was simple, an oversized flannel shirt, sometimes worn over a t-shirt, and baggy, worn out jeans to give an overall, dishevelled, appearance. The clothes were found ideally in charity shops or at the back of "Dad's wardrobe". A pair of Doc Martens or Converse shoes finished the ensemble.

Nirvana's lead singer Kurt Cobain epitomised the look with holes in his jeans and cardigan sweaters and the fashion world caught on when their second album, 'Nevermind' was released in 1991 and grunge made it onto the catwalk – specifically by Calvin Klein on an 18-year-old Kate Moss. Shrunken baby doll dresses, old prom dresses or even old petticoats and simple slip dresses appeared, often worn with chunky boots and for men, beanies, band t-shirts and knitted sweaters with patterns.

FRIENDS

For women, long loose hair was the most popular women's style, but the most requested hairstyle of the 1990s was said to be 'The Rachel'. Jennifer Anniston's character in 'Friends', Rachel Green, had the haircut people wanted – bouncy, layered, shoulder length, obviously styled to within an inch of its life yet at the same time artfully tousled.

HOODIES

Utilitarian styles such as cargo pants and The Gap's hooded sweatshirts became popular for everyday wear. Industrial and military styles crept into mainstream fashion and camouflage pants were everywhere on the street.

There was also a concerted move towards logoed clothing such as by Tommy Hilfiger

LEISURE

THE GAMES CHILDREN PLAYED

The trend in the 90s was for more electronic, video and computer games but younger children still enjoyed many of the traditional past-times, and events in the 90s such as the FIFA World Cups and the Olympics, produced special collections which reignited interest in collecting 'stickers,' and filling albums.

Crazes were still all the craze too and it was digital pets like Tamagotchi, housed in their small, egg-shaped, handheld video game console that became the biggest fads of the end of the decade.

The Teletubbies caused a huge sensation in 1997, communicating through gibberish and designed to resemble real-life toddlers, they became a huge commercial success, the toy Teletubbies being the most demanded toy of 1997.

However, it was Sony's PlayStation which was the big innovation of the 90s. The first version was able to process games stored on CD-ROMs and introduced 3D graphics to the industry. It had a low retail price and Sony employed aggressive youth marketing. Ridge Racer was the classic motor racing game used in the launch and the popularity of this game was crucial to the early success of the PlayStation.

RESTORATION OF THE SPA

From being at the centre of society in previous times, the spa industry had declined so much that by the 50s, leading spas such as those at Buxton, Cheltenham and Tunbridge Wells had closed. The 1990s saw a simultaneous rise of increasing disposable wealth, and the popularity of a new concept of the spa, pure self-indulgence and pampering.

The need to pause and detox from time to time fitted nicely into the growth of a 'wellness' culture and the understanding of holistic wellbeing, treatments to soothe the mind, body and spirit. Wearing a luxurious white robe and slippers, lounging by a heated pool reading magazines and dipping from time to time into the whirlpools, a trip to the steam room or sauna before taking a light lunch and then unwinding to a fragranced oil body massage because, as L'Oreal had been saying since the 70s, "you're worth it!"

IN THE 1990s

WHERE WE WENT ON HOLIDAY

In the 90s, if we went on a foreign holiday at all, 26m of us in 1996, the norm was to go for just the one, two-week summer break. Booking with a Travel Agent in town or finding a cheap package deal on Teletext, we arrived at our destination with a guide-book, Travellers Cheques and a camera complete with film.

Our favourite places were Spain and France, many of us travelling on the cross-Channel ferries rather than on the budget airlines. Our other favourite hot spots were Belgium, Turkey, Egypt, Kenya and Tunisia.

Although the gap year began in the 1960s, it was in the 1990s when the idea became the 'thing to do' amongst the children of the new wealthy middle classes.

Many visited India, Pakistan and Nepal, Australia, Thailand, the USA and New Zealand being their favoured countries to visit.

Some did voluntary work in the developing nations, building schools and teaching children English.

The 90s saw plenty of new cruise ships being launched for what became a massive growth industry. New cruise lines were formed, and many existing lines merged and Royal Caribbean, Celebrity, Fred Olsen and Carnival, Disney, Silver Sea and Princess lines were all introducing, predominantly older people, to new places and entertaining them royally on the way.

For others, at the opposite end of the cruising scale, was the immensely popular, 'Booze Cruise'. The day trip across the channel to France to stock up on duty free wine and cigarettes.

MUSIC

1990 - 1994

1990 Elton John's **Sacrifice** was initially released as a single in 1989 but only reached No. 55 in the UK. In mid-1990, Radio 1 DJ, Steve Wright began playing it and it soon caught on with other DJs and when re-released as a double A-side single with **Healing Hands** it became John's first solo No 1 single remaining at the top for five weeks.

1991 Cher made the 1960s **Shoop Shoop Song (It's in His Kiss)** an international hit once again. **(Everything I Do) I Do It for You**, from the soundtrack of the film 'Robin Hood: Prince of Thieves' was sung by Bryan Adams and became a huge hit, the best-selling single of the year and stayed at No 1 for 16 weeks.

1992 Shakespeares Sister had their only No 1 UK single hit with **Stay** which stayed at the top for eight consecutive weeks.
The best-selling single of the year was Whitney Houston singing the song written by Dolly Parton, **I Will Always Love You.**

1993 **Pray** by Take That, written by Gary Barlow, was the first of twelve singles by the band to reach No 1 in the UK and the first of a run of four consecutive No 1's.

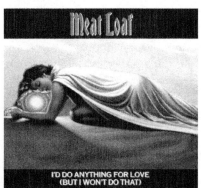

I'd Do Anything for Love (But I Won't Do That) was the song of the year and won Meat Loaf a Grammy Award for the Best Rock Solo Vocal Performance.

1994 The Most Beautiful Girl in the World by the unpronounceable Love Symbol, or 'The Artist Formerly Known as Prince' reached No 1.
The Manchester United football squad had the help of Status Quo, who wrote and sang along on their two week No 1 hit, **Come on You Reds.**

1995 - 1999

1995 Four artists had two No 1 hits this year. The Outhere Brothers with **Don't Stop (Wiggle Wiggle)** and **Boom Boom Boom**. Take That with **Back for Good** and **Never Forget** and Robson Green & Jerome Flynn with **Unchained Melody/ Bluebirds Over the White Cliffs of Dover** – the best seller of the year, and **I Believe/Up On the Roof.**

1996 This was a year with 23 No 1s. Most being at the top for only one week, but Fugees was No 1 twice with the same song **Killing Me Softly.** Firstly, for four weeks in June and then with a break for a week for **Three Lions (Football's Coming Home)** and another week in July.

1997 Elton John topped the charts for five weeks with **Candle in the Wind 1997**, a re-written and re-recorded version of **Candle in the Wind** as a tribute to the late Diana, Princess of Wales.
Another kind of tribute, this time to the popularity of the Teletubbies, their **Teletubbies say 'Eh-oh!'** stayed at No 1 for two weeks in December.

1998 The main soundtrack song from the blockbuster film Titanic provided Celine Dion with a hit, **My Heart Will Go On.**
Cher reinvented herself, and her song, **Believe** stayed at No 1 for seven weeks and was the year's best seller.

1999 Britney Spears made her debut single with **...Baby One More Time** which became a worldwide hit and sold over ten million copies.
Cliff Richard's **Millenium Prayer** is knocked off its 3 weeks at No 1 spot just in time for the boy band, Westlife, to make the Christmas No 1 with **I Have a Dream/Seasons in the Sun.**

In The 1990s

Cool Britannia

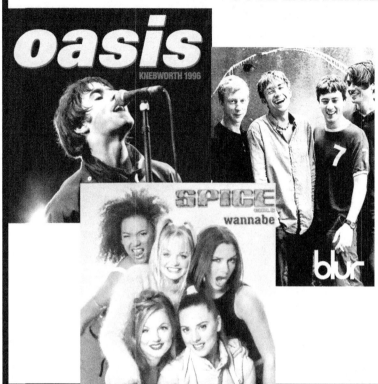

Throughout the mid and second half of the 1990s, Cool Britannia was a period of increased pride in the culture of the UK inspired by the 'Swinging London' of the 1960s pop culture. This brought about a huge success of 'Britpop' with groups such as Blur and Oasis and particularly, the Spice Girls.

Mel B, 'Scary Spice', Melanie C, 'Sporty Spice', Emma Bunton, 'Baby Spice', Geri Halliwell, 'Ginger Spice' and Victoria Beckham, 'Posh Spice' brought girl power to the fore. Their first single was 1996's iconic **Wannabe**, which established the group as a global phenomenon as 'Spice Mania' circled the globe. They scored the Christmas Number 1 single three years in a row and had nine UK No 1's in total.

Love Is All Around

In June 1994, Wet Wet Wet the Scottish soft rock band had a huge international hit, with 15 weeks as the UK No 1, with their cover of the 1960s hit by The Troggs, **Love Is All Around.** Their version was used on the soundtrack of the blockbuster film 'Four Weddings and a Funeral'.

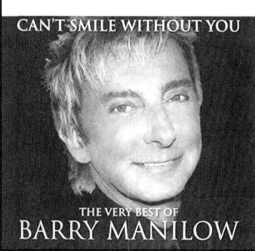

Richard Curtis, the director of the film, had approached Wet Wet Wet with a choice of three cover songs to record for the soundtrack, the other two being **I Will Survive** by Gloria Gaynor and Barry Manilow's **Can't Smile Without You**.

SCIENCE AND NATURE

THE HUBBLE TELESCOPE

The Hubble telescope is a general-purpose orbiting observatory. Orbiting approximately 380 mi (612 km) above Earth, the 12.5-ton Hubble Space Telescope has peered farther into the universe than any telescope before it. The Hubble, which was launched on April 24, 1990, has produced images with unprecedented resolution at visible, near-ultraviolet, and near-infrared wavelengths since its originally faulty optics were corrected in 1993.

Although ground-based telescopes are finally starting to catch up, the Hubble continues to produce a stream of unique observations. During the 1990s and now into the 2000s, the Hubble has revolutionised the science of astronomy, becoming one, if not the most, important instruments ever used in astronomy.

ADD TO BASKET

Mint Velvet Star Print Jumper, Pink

£69.00

Free Click & Collect over £30 & free returns
View delivery & returns options

Size: size guide

XS   S   M   L

XL

Add to your basket

♡ Add to wish list

ROYAL ALBERT OLD COUNTRY ROSES 40 PIECE DINNER TEA SET SERVICE TEASET ENGLAND

Condition: Used

Time left: 32m 7s | (13 Mar 2022 12:25:58 GMT)

Current bid: **£185.00**   [32 bids]

Bid amount

Submit bid

Enter £790.00 or more

♡ Watch this item

Posts from United Kingdom

The first ever shopper bought online from Tesco in 1984 using her television remote control, but it was in 1990s, following the creation by Tim Berners-Lee of the World Wide Web server and browser and the commercialisation of the internet in 1991 giving birth to e-commerce, that online shopping really began to take off.

In 1995, Amazon began selling books online, computer companies started using the internet for *all* their transactions and Auction Web was set up by Pierre Omidyar as a site *"dedicated to bringing together buyers and sellers in an honest and open marketplace."* We now know this as eBay and we can buy just about anything on Amazon.

Comparison sites were set up in 1997 and in 1998, PayPal was founded, the way to pay online without having to share your financial information. By 1999, online only shops were beginning to emerge and paved the way for 'Click for Checkout' to become commonplace.

IN THE 1990s

THE KYOTO PROTOCOL

In December 1997, at the instigation of the United Nations, representatives from 160 countries met in Kyoto, Japan, to discuss climate change and draft the Kyoto Protocol which aimed to restrict the greenhouse gas emissions associated with global warming.

The protocol focused on demands that 37 developed nations work to reduce their greenhouse gas emissions placing the burden on developed nations, viewing them as the primary sources and largely responsible for carbon emissions.

Developing nations were asked only to comply voluntarily, exempted from the protocol's requirements. The protocol's approach included establishing a 'carbon credits system' whereby nations can earn credits by participating in emission reduction projects in other nations. A carbon credit is a tradeable permit or certificate that provides the holder

SHOCK WAVES

A large earthquake, by British standards, occurred near Bishop's Castle, Shropshire on the Welsh Borders on 2 April 1990 at 13:46 GMT. With a magnitude of 5.1, the shock waves were felt over a wide area of Britain, from Ayrshire in the north to Cornwall in the south, Kent in the east and Dublin in the west.

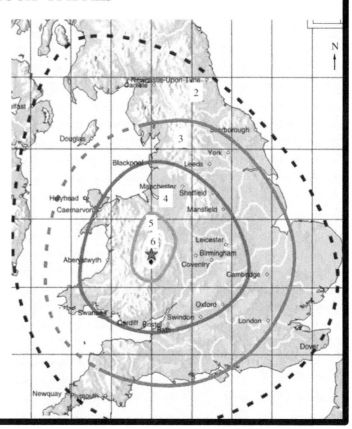

Worldwide in 1990, there were 18 quakes of magnitude 7.0 or above and 134 quakes between 6.0 and 7.0, 4435 quakes between 4.0 and 5.0, 2755 quakes between 3.0 and 4.0, and 8618 quakes between 2.0 and 3.0. There were also 29800 quakes below magnitude 2.0 which people don't normally feel.

The strongest quake was north of Pulau Hulawa Island in Indonesia, registering 7.8 on the Richter scale.

SPORT

1990 - 1994

1990 West Germany won the **FIFA World Cup** in Rome, defeating defending champions Argentina, 1–0 in the final.

The British golfer, Nick Faldo, had an amazing year, winning both the **Masters** and the Claret Jug at the **Open** at St Andrews, and capturing the PGA Player of the Year award, the first non-American to do so.

1991 At the **World Athletics** Championships in Tokyo, Mike Powell broke the 23 year-long world record **long jump** set by Bob Beamon, with a jump of 29' 4½".

1992 The rugby, **Five Nations Championship** is won by England who complete the Grand Slam for the second consecutive year.

The summer **Olympics** are held in Barcelona, Spain where Sally Gunnell takes home gold in the Women's 400 metres hurdles, Linford Christie triumphs in the Men's 100 metres, and rowers Matthew Pinsent and Steve Redgrave finish first in the Men's coxless pair, the first Olympic gold for all four athletes. In the **Paralympics**, Tanni Grey-Thompson in her debut Games, takes home four golds and a silver.

1993 Manchester United win the inaugural **English Premier League** title, their first league title in 26 years.

Shane Warne bowls the so-called 'Ball of the Century' in the first Test at Old Trafford. With his first ball against England, in his first **Ashes**, he bowled Mike Gatting out.

1994 Tiger Woods becomes the youngest man ever to win the **U.S. Amateur Golf Championships**, at age 18.

George Foreman becomes **Boxing's** oldest Heavyweight Champion at forty-five.

1995 - 1999

1995 In motor racing, Michael Schumacher wins his second consecutive **Drivers' Championship**, and Benetton wins its first and only Constructors' Championship.

British triple jumper Jonathan Edwards sets a world record in the **Athletics World Championships**, jumping 60' (18.29 m).

1996 The 95/96 **Rugby League** ends with Wigan declared champions.

Stephen Hendry wins the **World Snooker Championship** and remains the world number one.

1997 At 21, Tiger Woods becomes the youngest **Masters** winner in history, as well as the first non-white winner at Augusta. He set the scoring record at 270 and the record for the largest margin of victory at 12 strokes.

1998 In Japan, **Curling** is included in the Winter Olympics for the first time.

1999 Pete Sampras beats his biggest rival, Andre Agassi in the **Wimbledon Men's Singles** Final giving him his sixth win at the All England Club.

In the **US Open Tennis** final, at the age of 17, Serena Williams beats the number one player Martina Hingis and marks the beginning of one of the most dominant careers in the history of women's tennis.

In The 1990s

The Dangerous Side To Sport

By 1993, Monica Seles, the Serbian-American tennis player, had won eight Grand Slam titles and was ranked No. 1 in the world. On April 30, 1993, then just 19, she was sitting on a courtside seat during a changeover in a match in Hamburg when a German man, said later to be a fan of the tennis star's German rival, Steffi Graf, leaned over a fence and stabbed her between the shoulder blades with a knife. The assailant was quickly apprehended and Seles was taken to the hospital with a wound half and inch deep in her upper back. She recovered from her physical injuries but was left with deep emotional scars and didn't play again professionally for another two years.

Leading up to the 1994 Winter Olympics, figure skater Nancy Kerrigan was attacked during a practice session. This had been 'commissioned' by the ex-husband of fellow skater, Tonya Harding and her bodyguard. Kerrigan was Harding's long-time rival and the one person in the way of her making the Olympic team, and she was desperate to win. Fortunately for Kerrigan, the injury left her with just bruises – no broken bones but she had to withdraw from the U.S. Figure Skating Championship the following night. However, she was still given a spot on the Olympic team and finished with a silver medal. Harding finished in eighth place and later had her U.S. Figure Skating Championship title revoked and was banned from the United States Figure Skating Association for life.

Also in 1994, Andrés Escobar the Colombian footballer, nicknamed 'The Gentleman' - known for his clean style of play and calmness on the pitch - was murdered following a second-round match against the US in the FIFA World Cup. This was reportedly in retaliation for Escobar having scored an own goal which contributed to the team's elimination from the tournament.

In 1997, Evander Holyfield and Mike Tyson's fight made headlines after Tyson was disqualified for biting off a part of his rival's ear, an infamous incident that would lead to the event being dubbed "The Bite Fight".

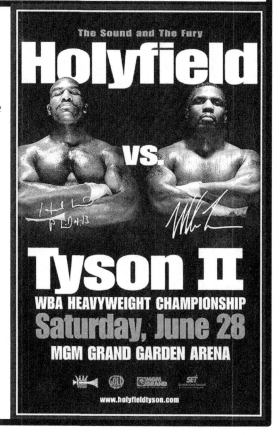

TRANSPORT

HAULAGE

The 1990s was a decade devoted to environmental considerations for haulage with top priority given to cleaner emissions and low noise levels. By the end of the decade, integrated IT solutions were being used to provide the tools necessary to increase efficiency and safety.

A significant factor in the 1990s was making the lorry more aerodynamic. A 20% saving in fuel consumption meant lower emissions and also the average transport operator could improve profits by up to 50%.

CRUISE SHIPS

The largest passenger ship of the 1990s was Royal Caribbean's 'Voyager of the Seas' at 137,276 gross tonnage and 310 m (1,020 ft) long.

This record was held between Oct 1999 and Sep 2000, when it was superseded by 'Explorer of the Seas', larger by only 12 GT. Royal Caribbean have, on order, and due 2024, an Oasis class cruiser of 231,000 gross tonnage, 362 m (1,188 ft) long.

THE HIGHWAY CODE

In July 1996 a separate written theory test was introduced to the Driving Test in the UK to replace questions asked about 'The Highway Code' whilst actually driving. Learner drivers were expected to know rather different information then from that published in the first edition of the Highway Code, price 1d, launched in 1931.

• In 1931 mirrors were not even mentioned.

• Drivers were advised to sound their horn when overtaking.

• At least 8 pages showed the various hand signals a driver should use. There was a single page in the current edition.

• Contained 18 pages (out of 24) of advice, compared to 135 pages in 2007.

• Included advice to drivers of horse drawn vehicles to 'rotate the whip above the head; then incline the whip to the right or left to show the direction in which the turn is to be made'.

It wasn't until the second edition of the Code that diagrams of road signs appeared, just 10 in all, plus a warning about the dangers of driving when tired or drinking and driving.

Renault Clio

Advertising for the first-generation Renault Clio introduced us to 'Nicole *et* Papa' and gave the small car a personality that appealed to drivers of all ages.

Ford Focus

The Focus replaced the previously very successful Escort. Ford wanted a 'World Car' to sell across all markets so the Focus was born and is still produced.

Toyota Previa

Toyota created the multi- purpose vehicle market with the Spacecruiser in the 80s, but the futuristic replacement, the Toyota Previa was a whole new approach to the people carrier.

Lexus LS 400

Toyota moved into the luxury market with the Lexus brand. The Lexus' flagship model is one of the most reliable vehicles ever built.

COCOTAXI

The auto-rickshaw began in Havana in the 1990s and soon spread to the whole of Cuba. These gas-scooters are named after their shape, that of a coconut and are made of a fibreglass shell with seats welded onto it. They can travel at about 30mph and because they are small, they weave and squeeze in and out of the city traffic. Blue Cocotaxis are for locals, yellow for tourists.

MOTORCYCLES

During the 1990s motorcycles started to evolve more quickly and there was a resurgence in the British biking industry with Triumph starting up production.

A bike lovers favourite however, was the 1995, Aprilia RS250.

NEW YEAR'S EVE 1999
The Millennium Bug

Whilst the world was getting 'ready to party' there was an undercurrent of anxiety about the Y2K (year 2000) Bug and many people were scared. When complicated computer programmes were first written in the 1960s, programmers used a two-digit code for the year, leaving out the "19." As the year 2000 approached, many believed that the systems would not interpret the "00" correctly, making the year 2000 indistinguishable from 1900 causing a major malfunction.

It was particularly worrying to certain organisations. Banks calculate the rate for interest owed daily and instead of the rate for one day, if the 'clocks went back' their computers would calculate a rate of interest for **minus** 100 years!

Airlines felt they were at a very great risk. All scheduled flights are recorded on computers and liable to be affected and, if the computer reverted to 1900, well, there were very few airline flights that year!
Power plants were threatened, depending on routine computer maintenance for safety checks, such as water pressure or radiation levels, the wrong date would wreck the calculations and possibly put nearby residents at risk.

Huge sums were spent to prepare for the consequences and both software and hardware companies raced to fix it by developing "Y2K compliant" programmes. Midnight passed on the 1 January 2000 and the crisis failed to materialise - planes did not fall from the sky, power stations did not melt down and thousands of people who had stocked up on food, water, even arms, or purchased backup generators or withdrawn large sums of money in anticipation of a computer-induced apocalypse, could breathe easily again.

The Millennium Dome

Officially called the O2, the huge construction and tourist attraction alongside the Thames in Greenwich, London was initially built to house an exhibition for the approach of the 21st Century. Designed by Sir Richard Rogers, the central dome is the largest in the world. On December 31, 1999, a New Year's Eve celebration at the dome was attended by some 10,500 people, including the Prime Minister, Tony Blair, and the Queen. Opening the next day, the Millennium Dome exhibition lasted until December 31, 2000.

AND A NEW MILLENNIUM

Memorabilia and Monuments

The Millennium Wheel Better known as the London Eye, at 135m (443 ft) it is Europe's tallest cantilevered observation wheel. Situated on the South Bank of the Thames when opened it used to offer the highest public viewing point in London until superseded in 2013 by the 245m high (804 ft) observation deck on the 72nd floor of The Shard.

Portsmouth's Millennium Tower opened five years late and officials were so concerned that people may actually have forgotten what the millennium was, that they gave it a new name, **The Spinnaker Tower**.

The Millennium Bridge is a steel suspension bridge for pedestrians over the River Thames linking Bankside with the City of London. Londoners nicknamed it the "Wobbly Bridge" after pedestrians experienced an alarming swaying motion on its opening day.

Lots of memorabilia was produced to mark the new millennium. Some pieces are timeless classics and others will soon be forgotten.

KEY EVENTS 2000-2009

2000:

Jan: Celebrations take place throughout the UK on the 1st and the Millennium Dome is officially opened by The Queen.

Aug 4th: Queen Elizabeth the Queen Mother celebrates her hundredth birthday

2001:

Feb: The Foot and Mouth disease crisis begins. Over 6 million cows and sheep are killed to halt the disease.

Jun: Labour wins the General Election. David Cameron is a new entrant, Edward Heath retires, and William Hague resigns as leader of the Conservatives.

2002:

Jan: The Euro is officially introduced in the Eurozone countries.

Jun: The Golden Jubilee. A special service is held in St Paul's Cathedral to mark the Queen's 50 years on the throne. Celebrations take place all over the country.

2003:

Mar: The United States, along with coalition forces primarily from the United Kingdom, initiates war on Iraq

May: BBC Radio 4 airs a report stating that the government claimed in its dossier, that Iraq could deploy weapons of mass destruction within forty-five minutes knowing the claim to be dubious.

Jul: Dr David Kelly, the weapons expert who was the reporter's source, is found dead.

2004:

Jan: The Hutton Inquiry into the circumstances of the death of Dr Kelly is published. The UK media, in general, condemns the report as a whitewash.

Jul: A new Countryside Code is published in advance of the 'Right to Roam' coming into effect in September across England and Wales.

TERRORISM

2001: On the 11th September, Al-Qaeda terrorists hijack civilian airliners and fly two into the Twin Towers of the World Trade Centre in New York, which collapse. There are 3,000 fatalities including 67 British nationals.

SOCIAL MEDIA

2004: In February, Mark Zuckerberg launches 'The Facebook', later renamed 'Facebook' as an online social networking website for Harvard University Students. In 2006 it was opened up to anyone over the age of 13.

21ST CENTURY

EXPLOSION

2005: On the morning of 11 December, the UK experienced its largest explosion since World War Two. A huge blast at the Buncefield fuel depot in Hemel Hempstead, was heard as far away as the Netherlands and caused the UK's biggest blaze in peacetime which shrouded much of south-east England in smoke.

HIGH SPEED TRAINS

2007: In November, the Queen officially opened 'High Speed 1' and 'St Pancras International' station. The Channel Tunnel first opened to Eurostar in 1994, with trains running from Waterloo, but the new 69-mile link meant the journey from London to Paris reduced to 2 hrs 15 minutes and to Brussels 1 hr 51 min.

2005:
Apr: Prince Charles marries Camilla Parker Bowles at a private ceremony at Windsor Guildhall.

Aug: Hurricane Katrina devastates much of the U.S. Gulf Coast from Louisiana to the Florida Panhandle killing an estimated 1,836 people

2006:
Jul: Twitter is launched, becoming one of the largest social media platforms in the world.

Nov: Alexander Litvinenko a British-naturalised Russian defector dies of polonium poisoning in London.

2007:
Jun: Tony Blair resigns as Prime Minister and Gordon Brown is elected unopposed.

Jul: England introduces a ban on smoking in enclosed public places in line with Scotland, Wales and N. Ireland.

2008:
Mar: Terminal 5 is opened at London Heathrow but IT problems cause over 500 flights to be cancelled

Nov: St Hilda's College admits male undergraduates and ceases to be the last single-sex college at Oxford.

Dec: Woolworths shuts down in the UK.

2009:
Jul: The largest haul of Anglo-Saxon treasure ever found, the Staffordshire Hoard, is first uncovered buried beneath a field near Litchfield. 4,600 items amounting to 11 lb of gold, 3lb of silver and 3.5k pieces of garnet cloisonné jewellery.

Oct: The independent audit of MPs expenses is completed and exposes a widespread parliamentary scandal.

KEY EVENTS 2010-2019

2010:

Jan: In the Chilcott Inquiry, set up in 2009, Tony Blair is questioned in public for the first time about his decision to take the UK to war against Iraq.

May: The General Election results in a Hung Parliament. An alliance is formed between the Tories and the Liberal Democrats.

2011:

Feb: An earthquake of 6.3 magnitude devastates Christchurch, New Zealand. Hundreds of people are killed.

Apr: Prince William marries Catherine Middleton in Westminster Abbey.

2012:

Jun: The UK begins celebrations of the Queen's Diamond Jubilee. Events include a pageant on the Thames and a Pop Concert outside Buckingham Palace

Jul: The summer Olympic Games are held in London, making it the first city to host them for a third time.

2013:

Jul: A new Marriage Act receives Royal Assent and same-sex marriage becomes legal in England and Wales.

Aug: A burger, grown from bovine stem cells in a laboratory, is cooked and eaten in London. The same month, a 15 ton 'fatburg' is removed after completely blocking a London sewer.

2014:

Mar: Prince Harry launches the Invictus Games for wounded soldiers.

Mar: The first gay weddings take place in England and Wales.

THE SHARD

2012: In July, The Shard, an iconic 'vertical city' is officially opened in London. It is the tallest building in Europe and the tallest habitable free-standing structure in the UK at 1,016ft (309.6 m)

THE ARAB SPRING

2010: 'The Arab Spring', a series of anti-government protests, uprisings, and armed rebellions spread across much of the Arab world. Starting in Tunisia it spread to Libya, Egypt, Yemen, Syria and Bahrain. Amongst leaders to be deposed was Gaddafi of Libya.

BREXIT

June 2016: After months of heated, angry argument and debate, the referendum on whether to leave the EU or remain within it, is held. Nearly 30m people take part and the result is to leave the EU: 51.9% votes to 48.1%.

March 2017: Article 50 is invoked and the two-year countdown to departure begins.

March 2019: Parliament rejected Theresa May's EU withdrawal agreement and a new deadline is set by The European Council to leave, with or without an Agreement, at the end of Oct 2019.

Jun 2019: Unable to 'deliver Brexit', Theresa May steps down and in Jul 2019: Boris Johnson becomes Prime Minister.

Oct 2019: The deadline to leave passes, and the EU agrees to a new date, end of Jan 2020. Commemorative Brexit coins are melted down.

Jan 2020: Johnson signs the Withdrawal Agreement.

January 31st 2020: At 11pm, the UK leaves the European Union and marks the moment with a party in Parliament Square.

2015:
Jan: Two Al-Qaeda gunmen kill 12 and injure 11 more at the Paris headquarters of the satirical newspaper Charlie Hebdo.

May: The General Election is won by David Cameron for the Conservatives with an outright majority of 331 seats.
Jun: The 800th anniversary of the Magna Carta.

2016:
Jun: The UK Referendum to leave the EU, Brexit, takes place and the majority vote is 'Yes'. David Cameron later resigns.
Jul: On July 14, Bastille Day (Independence Day), a terrorist drives a truck through a crowded promenade in Nice, France. 87 people are killed.
Nov: Donald Trump becomes US President.

2017:
There are a string of deadly terror attacks in Britain including : Westminster Bridge, the Manchester Arena and London Bridge.
Jun: The Tories lose their majority in Theresa May's general election gamble.

2018:
Apr: The UK, France, and United States order the bombing of Syrian military bases.

May: Prince Harry marries the American actress Meghan Markle in St George's Chapel, Windsor Castle. It is thought 1.9m people watched on TV worldwide.

2019:
Jun: Theresa May resigns as Prime Minister. Before she goes, she agrees a new legally binding target to reach net zero by 2050.
Jul: Boris Johnson becomes Prime Minister.

FILMS & THE ARTS

"One Ring to Rule Them All'

Based on the fantasy, adventure epics written by JRR Tolkein in the 1930s and 40s, Peter Jackson's trilogy of films became a major financial success, received widespread acclaim and is ranked among the greatest film trilogies ever made. The three films were shot simultaneously in Jackson's native New Zealand between 1999 and 2000 and with a budget of $281m, was one of the most ambitious film projects ever undertaken.

The **Lord of the Rings: The Fellowship of the Ring** was nominated for 13 Oscars and won four, one of which, unsurprisingly, was for the Special Effects as did **The Lord of the Rings: The Two Towers** and **The Lord of the Rings: The Return of the King**.

Peter Jackson then went on to make a further three films based on Tolkein's Middle Earth saga, **'The Hobbit: An Unexpected Journey**, **The Hobbit: The Desolation of Smaug** and **The Hobbit: The Battle of the Five Armies**. The three films were prequels to the Lord of the Rings saga and together, the six films became one of the 'greatest movie series franchise' of all time.

'The Greatest Fairy Tale Never Told'

In 2002, the Oscar for Best Animated Feature was awarded for the first time to **Shrek**, the large, surly, sarcastic, wisecracking, Scottish-accented greenish ogre with a round

face and stinky breath who took a mud shower outdoors near his home in the swamp and blew fart bubbles in a mud pool! But being a goodhearted ogre, children and adults alike, loved him!

'A Film of Our Times'

The Social Network made in 2010, is an American biographical drama portraying the founding of the social networking phenomenon Facebook and the resulting lawsuits. Based on the book, 'The Accidental Billionnaires' by

Ben Mezrich the film was nominated for the Oscars in 2011 winning The Best Adapted Screenplay but missing out on Best Picture to **The King's Speech**.

'Precious Pieces'

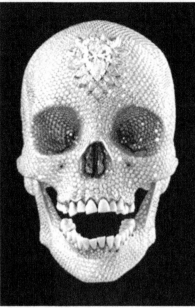

In 2007 Damien Hirst wowed the art-world with his fabulous **For the Love of God** a life-size platinum cast of an eighteenth century human skull, covered by 8,601 flawless diamonds, inset with the original skull's teeth. At the front of the cranium is a 52.4 carat pink diamond. The work is reputed to be the most expensive contemporary artwork ever made and was *allegedly* entitled **For the Love of God** in response to a question posed by the artist's mother "For the love of God, what are you going to do next?"! It has become one of the most widely recognised works of contemporary art and represents the artist's continued interest in mortality and the fragility of life.

Screaming Success

In May, 2012, a pastel version of **The Scream**, by Norwegian painter Edvard Munch, sells for $120m in New York City, setting a new world record for a work of art at auction.

'Question Everything, Believe Nothing'

Conspiracy theory is not a new phenomenon but in 2001, Dan Brown introduced the world to Robert Langdon and a whole new collection of conspiracies and secret societies, with his first book, **Angels & Demons**. Set in the Vatican and Rome, Langdon must decipher a labyrinthine trail of ancient symbols if he is to defeat the Illuminati, a monstrous secret brotherhood.

When **The Da Vinci Code** came along in 2003, hordes of tourists descended on Paris, staring at the Mona Lisa as though she held the secret to life and traipsing around cathedrals and monuments, speculating on the Holy Grail and obsessed with the Priory of Sion and Opus Dei.

By 2009 in **The Lost Symbol**, Brown had set his sights on the Capitol Building, Washington DC and the shadowy, mythical world in which the Masonic secrets abound.

Back in Italy in 2013, this time Florence, for **Inferno**, Langdon is also back to hidden passageways and ancient secrets that lie behind historic facades, deciphering a sequence of codes buried deep within Renaissance artworks with only the help of a few lines from Dante's Inferno.

The Top Ten UK Singles of the 21ˢᵗ Century

YEAR

2013   **Happy** by Pharrell Williams.

2002   Will Young's **Anything is Possible**

2013   **Blurred Lines** sung by Robin Thicke featuring TI and Pharrell Williams.

2014   Mark Ronson and featuring Bruno Mars with **Uptown Funk**

2011   Adele singing **Someone Like You**

2011   **Moves Like Jagger** by Maroon 5 featuring Christina Aguilera

2012   Gotye featuring Kimbra and **Somebody That I Used to Know**

2013   **Wake Me Up** by Avicii

2009   The Black Eyed Peas with **I Gotta Feeling**

2013   Daft Punk featuring Pharrell Williams and **Get Lucky**

First of the Century

The first No 1 Single of the 21ˢᵗ Century in the UK Charts is **Manic Street Preachers** with The Masses Against the Classes. This song by Welsh rock band was released as a limited-edition single being deleted, removed from wholesale supply, on the day of release. Despite this, it peaked at No 1.

Since 2014 streaming has counted towards sales, called "combined sales", at the rate of 100 streams equal to one download or physical purchase, although the singles chart no longer uses this ratio. The biggest selling song of the 21ˢᵗ Century, based on combined physical, download and streaming sales, *and as of Sep 2017*, is **The Shape of You** by Ed Sheeran, (2017) with sales of just over 3 m i l l i o n .

Millennial Music

What about the music the Millennials, born in the 80s and 90s, like to listen to? It may eventually fit just as well onto a "best songs of all time" playlist alongside the likes of The Beatles and The Supremes. These are some of the 21st-century pop songs that could stand the test of time and they are all female artists too!

Single Ladies (Put a Ring on It) by Beyoncé. **Umbrella** by Rihanna featuring Jay-Z. **Shake it Off** by Taylor Swift. **Toxic** by Britney Spears. **Rolling in the Deep** by Adele and **Firework** by Katy Perry.

However, those of from the 'Good Old Days' are not surprised to know, that in 2019, a US study found that golden oldies stick in millennials' minds far more than the relatively bland, homogeneous pop of today. A golden age of popular music lasted from the 1960s to the 1990s, academics claimed. Songs from this era proved to be much more memorable than tunes released in the 21st century.

FASHION

Music and fashion have been intertwined since the 1960s and nothing appears to be changing at the beginning of the 21st Century. The young will imitate their idols. Today though, designers are taking their inspiration from the past and bringing it back into the future, the new millennium fashion is a 'fusion' of the 60's, 70's and 80's, feeding our freedom to 'wear what we want, whenever we want'.

However, one major shift of emphasis will be the consumer's demand for environmental sustainability and social responsibility and to move away from 'fast, disposable fashion'. Fashion began moving at breakneck speeds in the 1960's, and the young wanted cheaply made clothing to follow these new trends. Fashion brands had to find ways to keep up with the ever-increasing demand for affordable clothing and this led to the massive growth in manufacturing being outsourced to the developing world, saving us millions of pounds in labour costs.

In the 21st Century we are aware of dreadful labour practices and the enormous amounts of waste. The industry will need to slow down for the customer mindful of how their clothes are made.

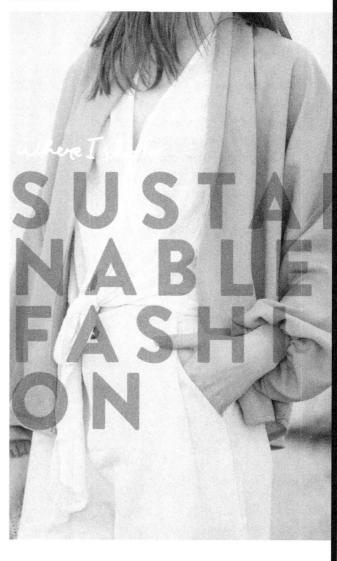

The Top Ten UK Singles of the 21st Century

YEAR	
2013	**Happy** by Pharrell Williams.
2002	Will Young's **Anything is Possible**
2013	**Blurred Lines** sung by Robin Thicke featuring TI and Pharrell Williams.
2014	Mark Ronson and featuring Bruno Mars with **Uptown Funk**
2011	Adele singing **Someone Like You**
2011	**Moves Like Jagger** by Maroon 5 featuring Christina Aguilera
2012	Gotye featuring Kimbra and **Somebody That I Used to Know**
2013	**Wake Me Up** by Avicii
2009	The Black Eyed Peas with **I Gotta Feeling**
2013	Daft Punk featuring Pharrell Williams and **Get Lucky**

Since 2014 streaming has counted towards sales, called "combined sales", at the rate of 100 streams equal to one download or physical purchase, although the singles chart no longer uses this ratio. The biggest selling song of the 21st Century, based on combined physical, download and streaming sales, *and as of Sep 2017*, is **The Shape of You** by Ed Sheeran, (2017) with sales of just over 3 million.

First of the Century

The first No 1 Single of the 21st Century in the UK Charts is **Manic Street Preachers** with The Masses Against the Classes. This song by Welsh rock band was released as a limited-edition single being deleted, removed from wholesale supply, on the day of release. Despite this, it peaked at No 1.

Millennial Music

What about the music the Millennials, born in the 80s and 90s, like to listen to? It may eventually fit just as well onto a "best songs of all time" playlist alongside the likes of The Beatles and The Supremes. These are some of the 21st-century pop songs that could stand the test of time and they are all female artists too!
Single Ladies (Put a Ring on It) by Beyoncé. **Umbrella** by Rihanna featuring Jay-Z. **Shake it Off** by Taylor Swift. **Toxic** by Britney Spears. **Rolling in the Deep** by Adele and **Firework** by Katy Perry.

However, those of from the 'Good Old Days' are not surprised to know, that in 2019, a US study found that golden oldies stick in millennials' minds far more than the relatively bland, homogeneous pop of today. A golden age of popular music lasted from the 1960s to the 1990s, academics claimed. Songs from this era proved to be much more memorable than tunes released in the 21st century.

21ST CENTURY

FASHION

Music and fashion have been intertwined since the 1960s and nothing appears to be changing at the beginning of the 21st Century. The young will imitate their idols. Today though, designers are taking their inspiration from the past and bringing it back into the future, the new millennium fashion is a 'fusion' of the 60's, 70's and 80's, feeding our freedom to 'wear what we want, whenever we want'.

However, one major shift of emphasis will be the consumer's demand for environmental sustainability and social responsibility and to move away from 'fast, disposable fashion'. Fashion began moving at breakneck speeds in the 1960's, and the young wanted cheaply made clothing to follow these new trends. Fashion brands had to find ways to keep up with the ever-increasing demand for affordable clothing and this led to the massive growth in manufacturing being outsourced to the developing world, saving us millions of pounds in labour costs.

In the 21st Century we are aware of dreadful labour practices and the enormous amounts of waste. The industry will need to slow down for the customer mindful of how their clothes are made.

2000 Tiger Woods wins the **US Open** golf by 15 shots, a record for all majors.

Australia wins the **Rugby League World Cup** against New Zealand. Italy joins the Five Nations **Rugby Union** making it the Six Nations.

2001 Sir Donald Bradman dies. He retains the highest **Test Match** batting average of 99.94.

Venus Williams wins the **Ladies Singles Final at Wimbledon**.

2002 "Lewis–Tyson: Is On". Lennox won the fight by a knockout to retain the **WBC Heavyweight Boxing** Crown.

Arsenal matched Manchester United with their third Double, **FA Cup** and **League title**.

2003 Mike Wier becomes the first Canadian and the first *left-handed golfer* to win the **Masters**.

Serena Williams beats her sister Venus in the **Ladies Singles Final at Wimbledon**.

2004 In Athens, Kelly Holmes wins **Olympic Gold** for the 800 & 1500m. Britain also win Gold in the 4x100m relay. Michael Schumacher, in his Ferrari, wins a record 12 of the first 13 races of the season, and wins the **F1** World Drivers Championship.

2005 Ellen MacArthur attains the World Record for **Sailing** the fastest solo circumnavigation of the globe. In **Cricket**, England win The Ashes.

2006 Justin Gatlin equals Powell's **100m world record** time of 9.77 seconds in Quatar.

In golf, Europe wins the **Ryder Cup** for the third straight time, defeating the USA 18½–9½.

2007 27 January – After nearly 50 years, the final edition of **'Grandstand'**, the BBC flagship sports programme is aired.

Australia completes a 5–0 whitewash over England in the **Ashes Series**, the first time since 1920–21 that one team has won all the Tests in the series.

2008 At the Beijing Olympics, Team GB dominate the **Cycling**, winning 14 medals, including 8 Gold.

Usain Bolt thundered to victory in the **100m Olympic final** at the Bird's Nest in a world record time. He also broke the world record in the 200m.

2009 Jenson Button and Brawn GP secure their first and only **F1 Drivers' Championship** and Constructors' Championship titles, respectively.

In an incident that shocked the entire sporting world, the **Sri Lankan cricket team** was attacked by terrorists while heading to the stadium to play a match.

2010 At his debut in the US, Amir Khan, the British boxer retains his **WBA Light Welterweight** title for the second time.

Alberto Contador of Spain, wins his 3rd **Tour de France** and 5th Grand Tour.

2011 Rory McIlroy fired a 69 in the final round of the **US Open**, breaking the record with a 268 and winning by eight strokes. He becomes the youngest US Open winner since Bobby Jones in 1923.

2012 At the **London Olympics** on 'Super Saturday', Jessica Ennis-Hill, Greg Rutherford and Mo Farah all win gold in an unforgettable 44 minutes inside the Olympic Stadium. On this one single day twelve British athletes win gold medals across six events

Bradley Wiggins wins the **Tour de France**, the first British rider ever to do so and Mark Cavendish wins the final stage on the Champs-Élysées for a record fourth successive year.

2013 The **Boston Marathon** is bombed by terrorists. At **Wimbldon**, Andy Murray defeats Novak Djokovic to become the first British winner of the **Men's Singles** since Fred Perry in 1936. He earns his second Grand Slam title

2014 The first ever Invictus Games is hosted in London with over 400 competitors from 13 nations. The FA Cup Final is won by Arsenal, a joint record 11th Cup having beaten Hull City 4-3 after extra time.

2015 In Golf, Jordan Spieth led from the start in the **Masters**, shooting a record-tying 270, 18 under, to win his first major at the age of 21. Later in the year he also wins the U.S. Open.

The **Grand National** at Aintree is won by 'Many Clouds' ridden by Leighton Aspell, his second consecutive Grand National Victory.

2016 Leicester City, 5,000-1 outsiders for the title, win the **Premier League.**

Former Leicester City player Gary Lineker stated that if Leicester won the league, he would present Match of the Day in his underwear!

2017 Roger Federer becomes the undisputed **King of Wimbledon** with his record 8th win.

Chris Froome wins his 4th **Tour de France**.

In the **Women's World Cup Cricket**, England beat India by nine runs in the final at Lords.

2018 The **Tour de France** general classification was won by Geraint Thomas of Team Sky, his first win.

Roger Bannister, the first man to run a four-minute mile died this year.

2019 At the **Cheltenham Festival**, 'Frodon' ridden by Bryony Frost wins the Ryanair Chase. She is the first woman to ride a Grade One winner at Cheltenham.

Tiger Woods wins his first major in 11 years at the **Masters**.

2020 At the Tokyo Olympics, Lamont Jacobs wins the **100m** sprint and is the new **'World's Fastest Man'**.

1947: Britain was struck this year by 'the perfect storm'. Record snowfall followed by a sudden thaw which culminated in heavy rain produced what is widely considered to be Britain's worst flood. Over 100,000 homes were directly affected and over 750,000 hectares of farmland submerged. The damages at the time totalled around £12 million, £300 million in today's terms.

1952: In August, the tiny village of Lynmouth, north Devon, suffered the worst river flood in English history. On the 15th, just over 9in (230mm) of rain fell over north Devon and west Somerset. The East and West Lyn rivers flooded and tons of water, soil, boulders and vegetation descended over Exmoor to meet at sea level in Lynmouth. The village was destroyed. The West Lyn rose 60 ft (18.25 m) above the normal level at its highest point and 34 people lost their lives.

1953: The great North Sea flood of January caused catastrophic damage and loss of life in Scotland, England, Belgium and The Netherlands and was Britain's worst peacetime disaster on record claiming the lives of 307 people. There were no severe flood warnings in place and the combination of gale-force winds, low pressure and high tides brought havoc to over 1,000 miles of coastline and 32,000 people were displaced because of flooding.

1963: Britain had the coldest winter in living memory, lasting for three long months from Dec 1962. The 6th March 1963 was the first morning of the year without frost anywhere in Britain.
It was so cold that rivers, lakes and even the sea froze over. On 25 February a record low of -22c in Braemar was recorded and 95,000 miles of road were snowbound.

1987: The Hurricane that wasn't supposed to be! Weatherman Michael Fish, like other forecasters, didn't see it coming. Eighteen people died and over 15 million trees were lost when in October, the hurricane-force winds blasted through south-east England. Meteorological research revealed a completely new weather phenomenon called the 'sting jet', a 100mph wind, the first to be documented in Britain.

WEATHER

2003: In August a new UK record was set for the 'Hottest Day in History' when temperatures reached 38.5c (101.3f) in Faversham, Kent. By the end of the summer, the heat had claimed the lives of over 2,000 people in Britain, mostly through heat stroke or dehydration.

An almost empty reservoir

1976: Britain had its hottest three months in living memory and it should have been the perfect summer, but with the continued sunshine came the worst drought in 150 years. Rivers dried up, soil began to crack and water supplies were on the verge of running out in Britain's most dramatic heatwave of the 20th Century. The drought was so rare, Britain appointed its first ever minister for drought, Denis Howell. He was nicknamed the minister for rain as the day after they installed him the heavens opened for the next two months!

2000: Following a wet spring and early summer, the autumn was the wettest on record for over 270 years. Repeated heavy rainfall in October and November caused significant and extensive flooding, inundated 10,000 homes and businesses. Train services cancelled, major motorways closed, and power supplies disrupted.

2007: Summer 2007 was the wettest on record with 414.1mm of rain falling across England and Wales in May, June and July - more than at any time since records began in 1766.
Although the rain was exceptionally heavy, climatologists say it was not the result of global warming. A report by the Centre for Ecology and Hydrology concluded the rain was a freak event, not part of any historical trend.

2004: A flash flood submerged the Cornish village of Boscastle during the busy holiday period when over 60 mm of rain (typically a month's rainfall) fell in two hours. The ground was already saturated due to two weeks of above average rainfall and the Jordan and Valency rivers burst their banks causing about two billion litres of water to rush down the valley straight into Boscastle. This led to the flash flood which caused total devastation to the area, but miraculously, no loss of life.

GLOBAL DISASTERS OF
Australian Bush Fires

Australia experienced the worst bushfire season ever in 2019-2020 with fires blazing for months in large parts of the country. Around 126,000 square kilometres of land and thousands of buildings were destroyed and at least 33 people died. Victoria and New South Wales were the worst affected and a state of emergency was declared in the capital city, Canberra.

Australia is used to bushfires, they are a natural part of the country's summer and native trees like eucalyptus need the heat for their seeds to be released, but this season they started earlier than usual, spread much faster, burned hotter and lasted longer, from June 2019 until March 2020, with the worst of the fires happening in December and January.

2019 was Australia's hottest and driest year on record with temperatures hitting 40c and above in every state and these hot, dry and windy conditions made the fires bigger and more intense than normal.

THE INDIAN OCEAN TSUNAMI

In the early morning of December 26, 2004, there was a massive and sudden movement of the Earth's crust under the Indian Ocean. This earthquake was recorded at magnitude 9 on the Richter Scale and as it happened under the ocean, the sea floor was pushed upwards, by as much as 40m, displacing a huge volume of water and causing the devastating tsunami which hit the shores of Indonesia, Sri Lanka, India, Thailand, and the Maldives.

Within 20 minutes the waves, reaching 30 feet high, and racing at the speed of a jet aircraft, engulfed the shoreline of Banda Aceh on the northern tip of Sumatra, killing more than 100,000 people and pounding the city into rubble. Then, moving on to Thailand, India and Sri Lanka, an estimated total of 250,000 people were killed, including many tourists on the beaches of Thailand. Millions more people were displaced, and eight hours later, and 5,000 miles from its Asian epicentre, the tsunami claimed its final casualties on the coast of South Africa.

Hurricane Katrina

Hurricane Katrina hit the coast of Louisiana on 29th August 2005. A Category 3 storm, it caused destruction from central Florida to Texas, but most lives were lost, and damage caused in New Orleans. It passed over Miami where the 80mph winds uprooted trees and killed two people. Hurricanes need warm ocean water to keep up speed and strength, so Katrina weakened whilst over the land to a tropical storm. Crossing back into the Gulf of Mexico, it quickly regained hurricane status and at its largest, was so wide, its diameter stretched

right across the Gulf. Katrina crossed back over the coast near Biloxi, Mississippi, where winds were the strongest and damage was extensive. However, later that morning, the first of 50 old levees broke in New Orleans, and a surge of floodwater poured into the low-lying city.

COVID 19 A GLOBAL PANDEMIC

The first human cases of COVID-19, the coronavirus disease caused by SARS CoV-2, were first reported from Wuhan City, China, in December 2019. Environmental samples taken in a food market in Wuhan where wild and farmed animals were traded, were positive for the virus and it is still unconfirmed whether the market was the origin of the virus or was just the setting for its initial spread.

The virus spread rapidly throughout China and has been found in 202 other countries, reaching Britain, from Europe, in late January 2020 and in March, the 'Stay at Home Order' or lockdown, was introduced. Non-essential travel was banned, schools were shut along with many businesses and venues. We were told to stay 6ft apart from others, self-isolate and, if at risk, to shield.

HOW ATTITUDES HAVE CHANGED

SEX AND SEXISM SELLS

Attitudes towards many aspects of our lives have changed significantly since the 1970s. One very entertaining way to see some of these changes is to look at the advertisements of the times.

Smirnoff made fun of the feminism movement in the 1970s.

1971: Change was about to happen, 'Because I'm Worth It' reflected women's rights, encouraging women to embrace their ambitions fearlessly and believe in their self-worth every day.

There can still be subtle sexism in adverts today. Research is showing that when people are portrayed in general, not just men or women, in non-stereotypical ways the ads perform better.

HOW ATTITUDES HAVE CHANGED

SIZE MATTERS

In Great Britain, cars were smaller in the 70s than they are now. A four-seater, just big enough for you, the family and a couple of suitcases was the norm, you didn't have to squeeze into parking spaces and there was no need to dread driving down country lanes. By the 21st Century, cars have become bigger and the ubiquitous SUV is everywhere. Even the not-so Mini Cooper has evolved since lorry drivers struggled to see the car in their side view mirrors and is now 61% bigger than the original.

The major reasons for the increase in size are firstly, they are produced abroad and therefore not designed with the British roads in mind; safety considerations such as airbags and crumple zones need more room to accommodate; manufacturers can charge more for a larger car whilst the cost of producing it is not much more than producing a small car and finance deals have removed the necessity of finding the cash up front and enable the purchase of bigger, luxury, models.

THE MINI THEN
Length 120ins Width 50ins Weight 580Kg

THE MINI 60 YEARS LATER
Length 150ins Width 68ins Weight 1150Kg

THE FORD FIESTA THEN
Length 140ins Width 62ins Weight 750Kg

THE FORD FIESTA 60 YEARS LATER
Length 160ins Width 69ins Weight 1200Kg

In just 50 years cars have become longer, wider and much heavier. The Mini has doubled in weight, the Fiesta is 60% heavier and SUV versions of a car are wider and heavier than their saloon counterparts. SUVs are very popular but use more fuel and have more emissions than the non SUV versions.

SUV electric cars use more electricity than non SUVs, and are more expensive to buy.

TOWARDS CARS

THE BMW 3 SERIES THEN
Length 171ins Width 63ins Weight 1100Kg

THE BMW 3 SERIES SUV 60 YEARS LATER
Length 185ins Width 74ins Weight 1885Kg

THE ROLLS ROYCE CULLIAN OF 2023
Length 210ins Width 80ins Weight 2739Kg

HOW IN CAR TECHNOLOGY HAS CHANGED

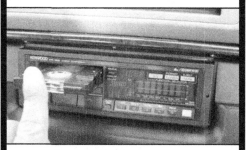

The 70s introduced the in-car cassette tape player

The 80s brought the CD-Radio player

The 90s brought in car telephones

The 2020s brought in self driving cars

And the future? Manufacturers are already working on making displays that respond to gestures, no touch screens necessary; you will be able to start your car or open the boot with your fingerprint and all the information you might need will be displayed on 'smart glass' in your windscreen!

HOW ATTITUDES HAVE CHANGED

It is a truth now universally acknowledged that smoking is bad for your health, but it wasn't always so. Cigarettes had been promoted as 'healthy', socially improving and fun! Some brands kept customer loyalty by offering gift vouchers.

As early as 1950 a report in the British Medical Journal had suggested a link between smoking and lung cancer and by 1962 the Royal College of Physicians had enough evidence to push for a ban on advertising.

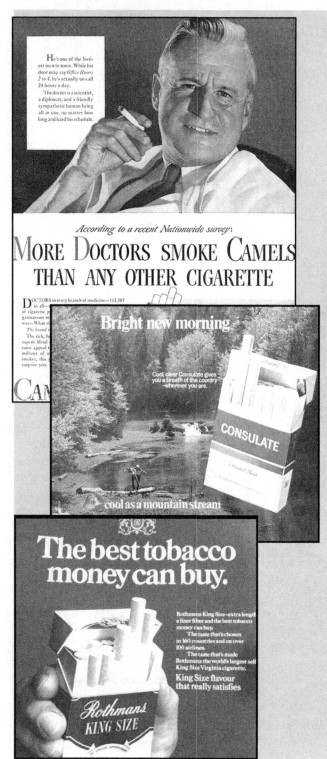

TOWARDS SMOKING

TIME LINE OF LAW CHANGES

1965: Television Commercials Banned

1971: All cigarette packets required a warning stating "WARNING by H.M. Government, SMOKING CAN DAMAGE YOUR HEALTH".

1982: The British Medical Association requested a ban on all forms of tobacco advertising.

1986: In 1986 adverts were banned in cinemas and it wasn't permitted to show a person smoking in an ad for any product or service.

1987: Smoking and cigarette advertising is banned on the underground – but more for safety reasons than those of health.

1991: The EU stated that all cigarettes must have two warnings on the packet, one on the front stating 'TOBACCO SERIOUSLY DAMAGES HEALTH' and another warning on the back such as "Smoking clogs the arteries and causes heart attacks and strokes".

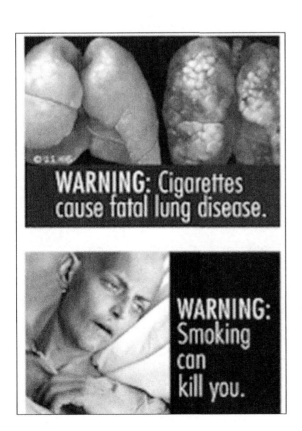

2002: The Tobacco Advertising and Promotion Act aims to wipe out tobacco advertising by 2005, including general advertising, promotions, sponsored events in the UK and sponsorship of global events including Formula 1 and snooker tournaments.

2003: Further EU sanctions made it illegal to brand cigarettes as 'mild' or 'light', and warnings on cigarette packets are enlarged; one covering at least 30% of the packet has to state either 'Smoking Kills' or 'Smoking seriously harms you and others around you'.

2003: The British government invest £31 million in *anti*-smoking campaigns.

2007: It becomes illegal to smoke in public places in the UK such as bars, restaurants and shopping centres and the legal age limit for purchasing tobacco was raised by two years to 18, however the minimum age for possession remained 16

HOW ATTITUDES HAVE CHANGED

It is a truth now universally acknowledged that smoking is bad for your health, but it wasn't always so. Cigarettes had been promoted as 'healthy', socially improving and fun! Some brands kept customer loyalty by offering gift vouchers.

As early as 1950 a report in the British Medical Journal had suggested a link between smoking and lung cancer and by 1962 the Royal College of Physicians had enough evidence to push for a ban on advertising.

TOWARDS SMOKING

TIME LINE OF LAW CHANGES

1965: Television Commercials Banned

1971: All cigarette packets required a warning stating "WARNING by H.M. Government, SMOKING CAN DAMAGE YOUR HEALTH".

1982: The British Medical Association requested a ban on all forms of tobacco advertising.

1986: In 1986 adverts were banned in cinemas and it wasn't permitted to show a person smoking in an ad for any product or service.

1987: Smoking and cigarette advertising is banned on the underground – but more for safety reasons than those of health.

1991: The EU stated that all cigarettes must have two warnings on the packet, one on the front stating 'TOBACCO SERIOUSLY DAMAGES HEALTH' and another warning on the back such as "Smoking clogs the arteries and causes heart attacks and strokes".

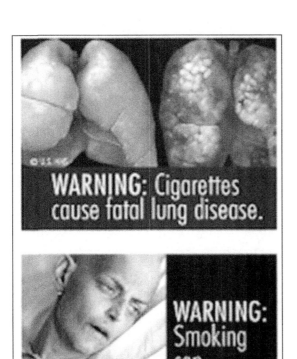

2002: The Tobacco Advertising and Promotion Act aims to wipe out tobacco advertising by 2005, including general advertising, promotions, sponsored events in the UK and sponsorship of global events including Formula 1 and snooker tournaments.

2003: Further EU sanctions made it illegal to brand cigarettes as 'mild' or 'light', and warnings on cigarette packets are enlarged; one covering at least 30% of the packet has to state either 'Smoking Kills' or 'Smoking seriously harms you and others around you'.

2003: The British government invest £31 million in *anti*-smoking campaigns.

2007: It becomes illegal to smoke in public places in the UK such as bars, restaurants and shopping centres and the legal age limit for purchasing tobacco was raised by two years to 18, however the minimum age for possession remained 16

HOW ATTITUDES HAVE CHANGED

FROM CORNER SHOP TO SUPERMARKET

There have been major changes to the British diet since the 1970s and by the 21st century, the story of the modern British dinner table is less home cooking, more prepared and takeaway meals; less fish and chips and vastly more meals reflecting our changing culture - more Italian, Indian, SE Asian and North American 'fast food'.

We shop differently. In the 1970s we bought meat at the butcher, fish at the fishmonger, fruit and vegetables at the greengrocer but now 85% of our grocery shopping is at the supermarket and 14% of that is on line. Supermarkets carry a huge range of products including previously unknown salad leaves, spices, exotic fruit and vegetables.

The move towards ever faster food continued. In 1980, the average meal took one hour to prepare. By 1999, that had dropped to 20 minutes. This change was driven by the increasing number of working women and the availability of ready meals. Between 1974 and 2014 "ready meals and convenience meat products" went up five fold.

More people were living on their own, further fuelling the market for fast food. This is matched by a drop in the popularity of fresh, canned and tinned food. The amount of canned peas bought dropped by two thirds between 1974 and 2014. Purchases of white bread have dropped 75% while those of brown and wholemeal bread have risen by 85%. Consumption of eggs peaked in the 1960s and has been declining ever since. Bananas replaced apples as the most popular fruit in 1996. There has been a 30% reduction in fresh vegetables and fruit, we buy many fewer carrots, turnips, parsnips, cabbages and sprouts.

Offal has fallen out of favour among younger, more squeamish Britons. In 1974 a typical household bought 36g of liver per week, but by 2014 the figure had fallen to just 3g - a 92% drop. Pork and mutton also saw more modest falls in popularity, while consumption of uncooked chicken and minced beef rose 62% and 35% over the same period respectively.

TOWARDS OUR FOOD

BURGERS, CHIPS AND PIZZA

Dried and fresh pasta was not even recorded on the National Food Survey until 1998. Between then and 2014, weekly household purchases in this category more than doubled. Pizza rose even more dramatically, with an average purchase from 2g per week in 1975 to 53g in 2014.

The number of takeaway pizzas bought per household shot up 1,000% over the same period. Burgers came to Britain in the 1970s and we eat 2.5 billion beef burgers a year. That roughly works out at the average Brit eating 37 burgers annually. A study of 2,000 adults also found 83% of those who eat meat and fish couldn't 'live' without them.

The nation still loves chips. Sales were three times higher in 2014 than in 1974. However, households reported buying a third less takeaway chips over the same period and the traditional accompaniment has fared differently. In 1974 we bought 44g of white fish - fresh, chilled or frozen - per week and while it is still the most popular fish choice, we buy just 19g a week.
Other types of seafood has done better. Shellfish purchases rose five fold, and those of salmon by 550%.

Consumption of the UK's preferred hot drink, tea, has declined steadily since 1974, from 68g per week to 25g. However, tea remains more popular than instant coffee, cocoa and malted drinks, and the decline has been attributed to "the coffee culture in the UK" and the decline in popularity of sweet biscuits! We drink 12 times as much bottled water now as we did in the 1980s. Skimmed and semi-skimmed milk overtook whole-fat milk in the 1990s and British households now drink four times as much.

HOW ATTITUDES HAVE CHANGED

MORE IS BETTER

'More was certainly better' in the decades following the war and particularly for children. School meals were a way of providing a hot, nutritious meal for every child and free school milk was given out every day to provide all important calcium. In the 1970s, school dinners were 'balanced', typically meat or fish and two veg. Fish and chips with peas or liver and mash with greens, followed by jam roly-poly with custard or

rice pudding. Yet this new prosperity was something of a poisoned chalice in relation to the health of the population, obesity was first recognised as a 'hazard to health' in the UK in 1976. Things became worse in 1980 when The Education Act abolished the minimum nutritional standards for school meals and removed the statutory obligation to provide meals for all children.

A 1970s school meal - main course

A 1990s school meal of Turkey Twizzlers, Smiley potato and beans with a sweet dessert

By the 2000s there was a push towards healthier food in schools and turkey twizzlers disappeared from the school canteen, being replaced with options such as fish curry, bean wraps, pasta dishes and salads. However, the trend was still for more and faster food, snacking continued to rise and the intake of fruit and vegetables declined.

The introduction of commercial tendering for school meals resulted in private companies bringing in 'a free-choice, cafeteria system'. The result - the easy option of burgers, chips and chocolate cake. Our children were being fed high calorie, junk food.

A modern day school meal of lasagna, vegetables with fruit and yogurt.

TOWARDS NUTRITION

TOO MUCH CAN BE BAD

As the 21ˢᵗ Century unravels before us, obesity levels are on a meteoric rise. The most obvious explanation for this is that we are a lot less active now than we were in the 70s. We walk a lot less and do less physical work. We snack more and consume a growing number of calories from sugary drinks, crisps and chocolate. We eat more processed foods and ready meals which are still high in sugar and salt. Computers, diet, TV and an 80% reduction in exercise at school, as it no longer holds the importance in the children's week, has contributed to childhood obesity. In the 2010s, the rise of the smartphone had a huge impact on our eating and health habits. Fast food delivery became available literally at our fingertips and online streaming

meant we could spend hours on the sofa bingeing on our favourite television shows. During the Covid 19 'lock downs', whilst gyms closed and people worked from home, ordering fast food or cooking lavishly at home became one of the few remaining pleasures to enjoy.

However, we *are* more aware of the issue of obesity and unhealthy lifestyles. Foods carry nutritional information on their packages, salt and sugar content has been reduced in processed food and thanks to public opinion, McDonalds provide salads, 'bottomless' fizzy drinks are no longer the norm and restaurants are obliged to add a calorie count to their menus

Crispy Chicken Salad

1092 kJ | 261 kcal

Freshly prepared salad with chicken breast in a crispy coating, lettuce, cucumber, sliced tomato

---

BURGERS

Hamburger
255 Calories
10g Fat
29g Carbs
13g Protein

Cheeseburger
300 Calories
13g Fat
30g Carbs
15g Protein

Double Cheeseburger
410 Calories
21g Fat
30g Carbs
24g Protein

Bacon Cheeseburger
340 Calories
16g Fat
30g Carbs
18g Protein

Bacon Double Cheeseburger
450 Calories
25g Fat
31g Carbs
27g Protein

Whopper Jr.
335 Calories
19g Fat
30g Carbs
15g Protein

The best news is, our average life expectancy is much better than it was. In 1970, the average person was expected to live to 72, while today that has increased to 81.

HOW ATTITUDES HAVE CHANGED

HOME WORKING

50 years ago, "going to work" meant heading to a physical location outside of your home and working there until 5pm. Today, your spare bedroom or dining room is just as likely to be your office. 43% of workplaces allow employees to work from home at least part of the time. If you DO go to the office, rather than wearing a suit or dress, you are more likely to be wearing jeans and trainers!

COMMUNICATIONS

Back in the 1970s, if you wanted to get in touch – faster than writing a letter and posting it - with a friend, you rang them up on a land-line phone and asked how they were doing. Now, we can see what our friends are up to on their social media. How their relationships are going, where they go on holiday, and, in some cases, what they had for breakfast. Information that used to take time to convey, is now delivered in a second by text or app.

24 HOUR NEWS

Half a century ago, if you wanted to find out what was happening in the world, you'd have to wait for the morning paper to come out. Now the news is on television, websites and apps 24 hours a day. There are hundreds of television channels now, all running day and night. In the 70s the three channels, BBC1, BBC2 and ITV played the National Anthem at midnight and stopped broadcasting. The screens were blank until about six in the morning and of course, no 'catch up' or 'streaming' or 'television whilst you are on the go."

President Putin says Nato is an 'obvious threat' to Russia

TOWARDS GETTING THINGS DONE

INTERNET SHOPPING

No need now to go to the shop anymore, clothes, music, groceries – anything you can think of – is brought to you with a tap on your computer, tablet or smartphone.

Outsunny 3 PCs Metal Outdoor Gliding Rocking Chair With Tea Table Patio Garden Comfortable Swing Chair...
★★★★☆ ~ 8,521

Keter Eden Bench Outdoor Storage Box Garden Furniture, Beige and Brown, 140 x 60 x 84 cm

Garden Corner Sofa rattan Garden Furniture Patio Set Garden Entertaining Set Garden Rattan Furniture...
★★★★☆ ~ 27

MEETING AND DATING

Dating 50 years ago meant one of two things. You met someone you liked out in the world and exchanged numbers, or you had someone set you up.

Today, hundreds of potential partners are just a swipe away, thanks to the proliferation of dating apps. Marriage is no longer expected, families are smaller and getting older goes on for longer!

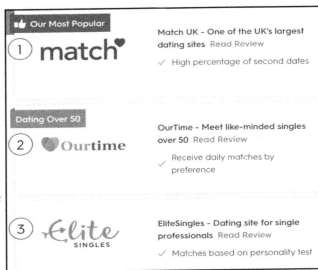

👍 Our Most Popular

(1) match♥

Match UK - One of the UK's largest dating sites Read Review
✓ High percentage of second dates

Dating Over 50
(2) ♥Ourtime

OurTime - Meet like-minded singles over 50 Read Review
✓ Receive daily matches by preference

(3) Elite SINGLES

EliteSingles - Dating site for single professionals Read Review
✓ Matches based on personality test

LEISURE

Board games, cards and dominoes have given way to computer games and virtual reality promises travel and other experiences without leaving your sofa! Everyone can watch whatever they want wherever they want on a phone, tablet or computer . You meet and speak with family and friends more via an app than by face to face. We watch more sport, but play less.

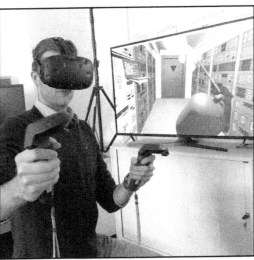

1975 CALENDAR

January
Su	Mo	Tu	We	Th	Fr	Sa
			1	2	3	4
5	6	7	8	9	10	11
12	13	14	15	16	17	18
19	20	21	22	23	24	25
26	27	28	29	30	31	

February
Su	Mo	Tu	We	Th	Fr	Sa
						1
2	3	4	5	6	7	8
9	10	11	12	13	14	15
16	17	18	19	20	21	22
23	24	25	26	27	28	

March
Su	Mo	Tu	We	Th	Fr	Sa
						1
2	3	4	5	6	7	8
9	10	11	12	13	14	15
16	17	18	19	20	21	22
23	24	25	26	27	28	29
30	31					

April
Su	Mo	Tu	We	Th	Fr	Sa
		1	2	3	4	5
6	7	8	9	10	11	12
13	14	15	16	17	18	19
20	21	22	23	24	25	26
27	28	29	30			

May
Su	Mo	Tu	We	Th	Fr	Sa
				1	2	3
4	5	6	7	8	9	10
11	12	13	14	15	16	17
18	19	20	21	22	23	24
25	26	27	28	29	30	31

June
Su	Mo	Tu	We	Th	Fr	Sa
1	2	3	4	5	6	7
8	9	10	11	12	13	14
15	16	17	18	19	20	21
22	23	24	25	26	27	28
29	30					

July
Su	Mo	Tu	We	Th	Fr	Sa
		1	2	3	4	5
6	7	8	9	10	11	12
13	14	15	16	17	18	19
20	21	22	23	24	25	26
27	28	29	30	31		

August
Su	Mo	Tu	We	Th	Fr	Sa
					1	2
3	4	5	6	7	8	9
10	11	12	13	14	15	16
17	18	19	20	21	22	23
24	25	26	27	28	29	30
31						

September
Su	Mo	Tu	We	Th	Fr	Sa
	1	2	3	4	5	6
7	8	9	10	11	12	13
14	15	16	17	18	19	20
21	22	23	24	25	26	27
28	29	30				

October
Su	Mo	Tu	We	Th	Fr	Sa
			1	2	3	4
5	6	7	8	9	10	11
12	13	14	15	16	17	18
19	20	21	22	23	24	25
26	27	28	29	30	31	

November
Su	Mo	Tu	We	Th	Fr	Sa
						1
2	3	4	5	6	7	8
9	10	11	12	13	14	15
16	17	18	19	20	21	22
23	24	25	26	27	28	29
30						

December
Su	Mo	Tu	We	Th	Fr	Sa
	1	2	3	4	5	6
7	8	9	10	11	12	13
14	15	16	17	18	19	20
21	22	23	24	25	26	27
28	29	30	31